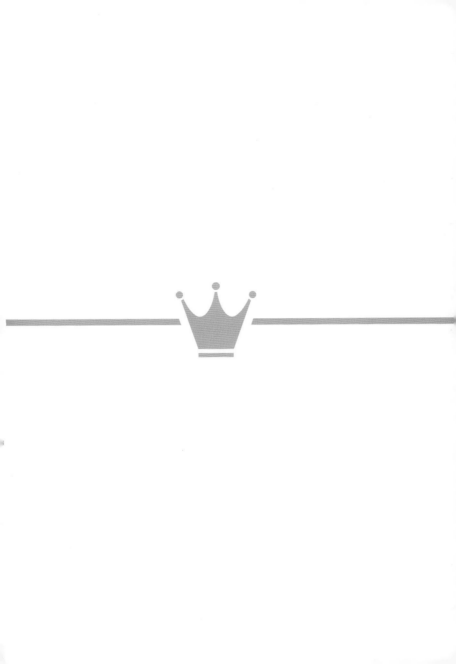

A STUDIO PRESS BOOK

First published in the UK in 2023 by Studio Press,
an imprint of Bonnier Books UK,
4th Floor, Victoria House, Bloomsbury Square,
London WC1B 4DA
Owned by Bonnier Books, Sveavägen 56, Stockholm, Sweden

www.bonnierbooks.co.uk

© 2023 Studio Press

3 5 7 9 10 8 6 4 2

All rights reserved
ISBN 978-1-80078-717-9

Written by Rachael Taylor
Edited by Stephanie Milton
Designed by Alessandro Susin
Picture Research by Paul Ashman
Production by Emma Kidd

This book is unofficial and unauthorised and
is not endorsed by or affiliated with Rolex

A CIP catalogue record for this book
is available from the British Library

Printed and bound in China

The publisher would like to thank the following for supplying photos for
this book: Alamy, Getty, Reuters, Shutterstock and Unsplash. Every effort
has been made to obtain permission to reproduce copyright material but
there may be cases where we have not been able to trace a copyright holder.
The publisher will be happy to correct any omissions in future printing.

ROLEX

The Story Behind the Style

RACHAEL TAYLOR

Contents

The World's Most Famous Watch Brand

Rolex has become shorthand for luxury. There is no watch you can strap on to your wrist that will be recognised for the status symbol it is quicker than a Rolex. And for many, this is the appeal.

Yet there was a time when the name Rolex – a word completely made up by the brand's founder Hans Wilsdorf – was not famous. It would take hard work, boundary pushing and a lot of self-belief on the part of Wilsdorf, a German orphan, to jettison the name into the upper echelons of horology; starting with convincing the pocket watch-wearing gentleman of the early 20th century that they wanted to wear the time on their wrist at all.

As you will discover, Rolex won its place in history by constantly questioning what was possible and innovating at all costs. It pioneered so many elements of watchmaking and design that are standard today, such as waterproof watches, placing a date window on the dial, and even removing the need to wind our watches.

It also found its way into some of the most exciting moments in history by placing Rolex watches on the wrists of adventurers and explorers. Its watches have travelled to the world's highest peaks and to the depths of the ocean; they have survived extremes of temperature, speed and pressure.

The story of Rolex is so much more than that of its watches. It is one of epic ambition and vision. What started out as a one-man band in London's Hatton Garden would become the epicentre of the Swiss watchmaking industry, and one of the most recognisable and coveted brands in the world.

ABOVE: A Rolex boutique in the GUM State Department Store on Red Square in Moscow.

An Orphan Who Became the King of Watchmaking

To tell the history of Rolex, we must start with a man rather than a watch. Hans Wilsdorf, who would go on to build what is arguably the world's most famous luxury watch brand, was born in the Bavarian town of Kulmbach, Germany, in 1881 to Anna and Johan Daniel Ferdinand Wilsdorf.

The Wilsdorfs owned an iron toolmaking business, which had been started by Hans Wilsdorf's grandfather. It was a successful enterprise that had provided a comfortable life for Wilsdorf, his older brother and younger sister. It was a happy and stable life until tragedy struck when Anna and Johan died months apart. By the time he was 12 years old, Wilsdorf was an orphan.

Anna's brothers stepped in to steer the children's fate, and it was decided that the toolmaking business that had belonged to their father should be sold to provide a financially stable future for them. Once this had been completed, the children were sent to elite boarding schools for the remainder of their childhoods. Wilsdorf was educated 45 kilometres away in Coburg, where he showed an interest in mathematics and foreign languages, becoming fluent in English.

Although this was an upsetting chapter in his life, Wilsdorf credits these events with giving him the strength of character

required to be successful in the future. In an autobiography he wrote as part of a series of four books titled *Rolex Jubilee Vade Mecum*, published in 1946, he reflected: "The way in which [my uncles] made me become self-reliant very early in life made me acquire the habit of looking after my possessions and, looking back, I believe that it is to this that much of my success is due."

Wilsdorf's first foray into the world of work was an apprenticeship with a pearl exporter in Geneva that sold to businesses across the world. The experience that he gained in this role would prove vital when setting up his own business, and he described it as being "invaluable throughout my career". One of the lessons learned was that it was possible to build a business around products others had made, which would be the founding idea for his initial watch business.

In 1900, Wilsdorf moved to La Chaux-de-Fonds, a town in the Jura mountains – an area of Switzerland that is synonymous with watchmaking. He took a job with major watch exporter Cuno Korten, which was his introduction to the world of horology. While his main role was corresponding with the English market, another of his duties at Cuno Korten was to keep its warehouses of pocket watches in working order. To do this, he had to manually wind hundreds of pocket watches each day. It seems little wonder after this experience that he would later become obsessed with the quest to create a self-winding watch movement. After two years in the Swiss mountains, Wilsdorf returned to Germany to complete mandatory military service. He did not return to Switzerland upon its completion in 1903 but instead moved to London and took a job with a watchmaker. He also met and married his first wife at this time, an English woman called Florence Crotty, and became a British citizen.

BOTTOM: A view of the caseback of a Rolex Oyster Perpetual, circa 1931.

Two years later, at the age of 24, Wilsdorf was ready to strike out on his own, and in 1905 he opened his own watch business in partnership with his brother-in-law Alfred Davis. The company, which had its offices at 83 Hatton Garden in London, was called Wilsdorf & Davis and specialised in sourcing Swiss movements and placing them within English-made cases.

At that time, pocket watches were the mainstream method of timekeeping. Wristwatches did exist but were not common, and were considered to be a women's accessory. Indeed, the first wristwatches were made for women, as their dress at that time didn't allow for the comfortable wearing of pocket watches, since they didn't have pockets.

Wilsdorf was a visionary in this respect. He believed in the potential of wristwatches, and correctly forecast that this smaller,

more wearable product would one day make the larger pocket watch obsolete. He set about trying to change the image of wristwatches.

A fundamental step was finding a manufacturer called Aegler in the Swiss town of Bienne that was making precision movements that could fit inside a wristwatch. Wilsdorf placed a large order, and soon Wilsdorf & Davis became one of the leading British wristwatch firms.

In a bid to establish his business as a brand rather than simply a dealer, Wilsdorf wanted to create a new name for the company; a catchy one that would look good on a dial and be easy to pronounce in many languages. He had experimented with many combinations of letters in search of this made-up name but failed to find anything that worked. Then, while riding through London's Cheapside on the upper deck of a horse-omnibus in 1908, it came to him. Or as he would later jest: "A genie whispered 'Rolex' in my ear."

Under this new name, Wilsdorf continued his quest to create reliable wristwatches with quality movements. In 1910, Rolex had a breakthrough when one of its products, powered by an Aeglar movement, became the first wristwatch in the world to receive the Swiss Certificate of Chronometric Precision – a mark of horological excellence. Four years later, another milestone would be achieved when the Kew Observatory in London awarded a Rolex wristwatch with a Class A precision certificate. This had previously only been given to marine chronometers used for navigation, and it further solidified the reputation of Rolex as a purveyor of precise timekeeping instruments.

In 1914, World War I broke out, and the following year the British government introduced a 33.3% customs duty as part of the war effort. By this time, Rolex's London office, which had a staff of 60 people, was exporting its watches all over the world and the tax change would make that difficult. As such, Wilsdorf made the decision to move the company to Bienne in Switzerland. It already had an office in La Chaux-de-Fonds, which it opened in 1917 for marketing purposes, but this move would remove it from the British watch industry altogether.

And, so, the legacy of Rolex's Swiss-made watches began, with the Swiss company Rolex S.A. registered in Geneva in 1920.

OPPOSITE TOP: A watchmaker assembles a Rolex movement in Bienne in 1942, a task that requires much dexterity.

OPPOSITE BOTTOM: A powerful microscope allows a watchmaker in Geneva in 1949 to take a closer look at a Rolex watch.

The Origins of the Oyster

With Rolex settled into its new home in Switzerland, the company continued to develop its watch offering with a focus on precision and durability, as well as building its brand. Though certainly catchy, the name Rolex had not become an overnight success. Tired of waiting for it to catch on, Hans Wilsdorf launched a major marketing campaign in 1925, pledging to invest at least £12,000 a year – nearly £1 million in today's money. He also increased the number of watches Rolex was producing with its own branding on the dial, as it has been producing both branded and unbranded watches up until that time.

A major leap forward for Rolex's brand was the launch of the Oyster in 1926. This new style of watch promised to be waterproof and dustproof thanks to a hermetically sealed case, proving its durability. It also made it an obvious choice for sporting activities, which would prove to be a rich source of marketing for Rolex in the years ahead.

The Oyster case had a patented system of screwing down the bezel, caseback and winding crown against the middle case to seal the movement inside securely. The winding crown, which is made from 10 individual parts, was key as it acted as a go-between between the sealed inner world of the case and its functional external elements.

The Oyster case would become the backbone of Rolex. Nearly every watch in its contemporary range features an Oyster case, and the names of all the models reference it. A Submariner is technically named an Oyster Perpetual Submariner and a GMT-Master II is an Oyster Perpetual GMT-Master II, and so on. The only exception is the 1908 dress watch, which does not have an oyster case.

Rolex's iconic fluted bezels are a throwback to the early Oyster cases. Although these flourishes are decorative now, the ridges originally served a purpose to allow a special tool to screw the bezel securely to the mid case.

OPPOSITE: A 1959 Rolex Oyster Perpetual on a brown alligator strap.

ABOVE: A close shot of a Rolex Oyster Perpetual dial and fluted bezel.

Rolex at War

Despite his German heritage, Hans Wilsdorf was a staunch opposer of the Nazi party, and during World War II he found an ingenious way to show his support to British troops. From his office in neutral Switzerland, he made it known that British soldiers could place an order for a Rolex watch and that payment would not be required until after the war.

It is believed that 3,000 soldiers ordered a Rolex during World War II, including many in prisoner of war camps in Germany. Requests could be made in writing via the International Red Cross and soldiers were allowed to pick any model.

One of the soldiers who ordered a watch was Flight Lieutenant Gerald Imeson. He was one of the men involved in the mass escape attempt from Stalag Luft III prisoner of war camp, which was later made famous by its depiction in

LEFT: The Rolex ref: 3525 that Flight Lieutenant Gerald Imeson wore as a prisoner of war in World War II.

OPPOSITE: Steve McQueen in character as Captain Virgil Hilts in the 1963 film *The Great Escape.*

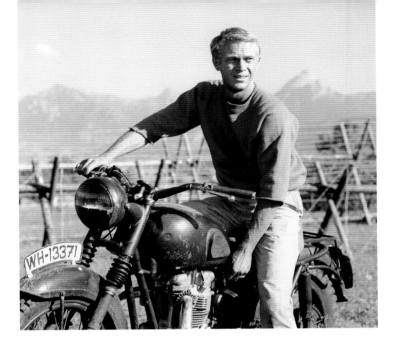

the 1963 film *The Great Escape*. As Imeson covertly shook soil collected from digging secret escape tunnels out of his trouser legs and onto the camp grounds, he did so with a Rolex Oyster Chronograph Ref. 3525 on his wrist. Sadly, Imeson was not one of the 76 soldiers who made it out, and his chronograph would accompany him on gruelling enforced marches through Germany as the Nazis tried to evade the Russians.

After the war, it was time for Rolex to collect. Although the watchmaker didn't chase a single invoice, it is said that every soldier paid. The families of fallen soldiers who had ordered a Rolex often attempted to settle the bill on their behalf. Imerson paid his £15 in 1947. The watch would later sell at auction via Christie's for £155,000 in 2022.

The 1950s

The 1950s was a prolific period for Rolex, during which it would create seven of its iconic models. The reason for such rapid innovation was that the Swiss watchmaker was chasing a new market for its timepieces by creating professional tool watches for specific sports or jobs. These were watches that would not just tell the time but could aid their wearer in some other way, too.

Rolex targeted activities on land, in the sea and in the air, including diving, climbing, aviation and exploration. This period would see the launch of the Explorer for adventurers, the Submariner and Sea-Dweller for divers, the Milgauss for scientists, and the Cosmograph Daytona for racing car drivers.

Although commercial versions of these watches would make it into the mainstream, each model genuinely started out

as an experimental timepiece designed for professionals. As such, most were put to the test in real-life situations, such as expeditions to Mount Everest. Chosen professionals would feed back information to the watchmaker, allowing it to improve the functionality of the timepieces.

Another launch during this decade was the Lady-Datejust, which was an important development of a different kind. It targeted another new audience for Rolex as the brand's first watch made specifically for women.

Rolex also launched its Day-Date model in the 1950s, which would prove to be one of its most sought-after timepieces and worn by many world leaders and celebrities. Such was its association with powerful men that it would pick up the nickname 'President'.

OPPOSITE: Adverts from the 1950s promoting Rolex's professional watches.

ABOVE: The Explorer series was a result of a flurry of innovation in the 1950s.

Rolex Oyster Perpetual 1035

Chronometer made in 18 carat gold only, "moiré" finish bezel with matching 18 carat gold "moiré" bracelet.

Rolex Oyster Perpetual 1013

Officially certified chronometer, selfwinding movement, guaranteed waterproof to 165 feet (50 m.), available in 18 carat gold only, with a variety of dials.

Explorer 1016

Worn by Sir John Hunt in his conquest of Everest, the Explorer is a specially robust version of the fabled Oyster. Officially certified chronometer. Guaranteed water-proof to 330 feet (100 m.). Stainless steel case. Highly luminous dial.

Explorer II 1655

Known as the "Explorer II" this chronometer is of particular interest for speleologists. It is equipped with a 24 hour hand and the very strong winding crown is further protected by a special shouldering.

The Crown

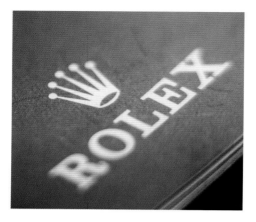

Perhaps just as famous as the name Rolex is the crown symbol that appears on all of its watches. In fact, for watch collectors, 'The Crown' is interchangeable with the brand's name when discussing Rolex.

The five-pointed Art Deco-style crown, which is also referred to as a coronet, was first trademarked by Rolex in 1925. The crown had two marginal redesigns, one in 1965 and a second in 2002. These tweaks enhanced and updated the silhouette and colour schemes, but as logos go the Rolex crown has been a fairly constant piece of branding since its conception.

The symbolism of using a crown to represent Rolex is to present its watches as markers of success that should be aligned with personal or professional milestones. As its marketing suggests: a crown for every achievement.

Today, you will find the iconic crown on Rolex's winding crowns as well as on the dial, positioned just above the word 'Rolex' or standing in place of a numeral at 12 o'clock. You will also see it littered through marketing and advertising material, as well as on boxes and in stores, and on many other items associated with the brand. Wherever there's Rolex, there's sure to be a crown.

PREVIOUS: A vintage catalogue showing Perpetual, Explorer and Explorer II models.

OPPOSITE: The crown branding embossed on documentation for a 2003 Datejust.

BELOW: Rolex's motif on the 18-carat gold winding crown of a Cellini Moonphase.

Moments in History

A spirit of adventure has always been at the heart of Rolex watchmaking, as well as a desire to test out its watches in extreme, real-world conditions. This has led to Rolex watches being present during some of the most famous moments in history.

When two soon-to-be-famous climbers scaled Everest, Rolex was there. When scientists plunged to the depths of the undiscovered Mariana Trench, Rolex was there. When the King of Speed broke the land speed barrier, Rolex was there.

And in every celebration of human endurance and accomplishment is a subtle reminder to the watch lover that its timepieces are not only capable of surviving the pressures of such quests, but that the adventurers themselves rely on Rolex to assist them.

LEFT: A view of Mount Ama Dablam in the Everest region of the Himalayas in Nepal.

Swimming the English Channel

Mercedes Gleitze was a long-distance swimmer born in Brighton, England, in 1900. She shot to fame when – after her eighth attempt – she became the first Englishwoman to swim the English Channel in 1927, completing the feat in 15 hours and 15 minutes.

Unfortunately, the triumph was tainted by Dorothy Cochrane Logan, who claimed less than a week later to have completed the same swim. She was exposed as a fraud, but this cast doubt on Gleitze's claim. Under pressure from the media, Gleitze offered to swim the Channel again to prove her innocence.

Rolex seized on the 'vindication swim' as a marketing opportunity to put the waterproofness of its Oyster case to the test. It asked Gleitze to wear an Oyster watch around her neck during the swim.

By the time she got back in the water, the temperature had dropped significantly. After more than 10 hours in cold water, Gleitze had to be pulled out after falling in and out of consciousness. The attempt had failed, but her resilience was enough to quiet naysayers and her original record remained intact. So too did the Oyster watch, and Rolex celebrated this achievement with a full-page advert in the London Daily Mail the next day. Rolex would continue to work with Gleitze in its marketing campaigns, making her the first ever Rolex ambassador.

OPPOSITE LEFT: Mercedes Gleitz preparing to set off from Folkestone for her seventh attempt to swim the English Channel.

OPPOSITE RIGHT: A photograph taken as Lord Clysedale and David McIntyre flew over Mount Everest on April 3rd, 1933.

The First Flight Over Mount Everest

With the Rolex Oyster proven at sea thanks to Mercedes Gleitze, Rolex looked to the skies. Captain Charles Douglas Barnard, who would go on to set records for long-distance aviation, was the first pilot to take the watch on a flight. He reported to have found it "eminently suitable".

In 1933, Lord Clydesdale and David McIntyre were planning their own aviation adventure as they prepared to attempt the first flight over Mount Everest, the world's highest peak at more than 9,000 meters (29,528ft) above sea level.

The aim was to conquer the feat, but also to get some ariel photographs. Lieutenant-Colonel Stewart Blacker joined Lord Clydesdale in his bi-plane, camera in hand and Rolex Oyster on his wrist. Blacker later said: "I can hardly imagine that any watches have ever been subjected before to such extremes."

Breaking Land and Air Speed Records

Sir Malcolm Campbell was a British journalist and racing motorist who had an obsession with speed. His passion for fast cars and boats would lead him to break several records for speed on land and water.

Campbell broke the land speed record for the first time in 1924, hitting 146.16mph at Pendine Sands in Wales. He would go on to break the world land speed record eight more times over the next decade. He achieved his final land speed record in 1935 at the Bonneville Salt Flats in Utah, USA, when he became the first car driver to exceed 300mph.

Campbell wore a Rolex Oyster during many of these drives but famously rejected payment from Rolex, which had offered him renumeration in exchange for testing the durability of its watch at high speeds. Despite this, he did provide a testimonial, writing: "I have now been using my Rolex watch for a while, and it is keeping perfect time under somewhat strenuous conditions." Rolex would later make a version of the Oyster with 'Campbell' printed on the dial.

Other thrill-seekers to wear a Rolex while breaking speed records included Chuck Yeager. In 1947, the US Air Force captain broke the speed of sound barrier wearing an Oyster when he flew a Bell X-1 rocket engine-powered plane at Mach 1.06 over the Rogers Dry Lake in the southern California desert. Another was stuntman Stan Barrett. He exceeded the speed of sound on land in 1979, hitting 739mph at Edwards Air Force base, where Yeager had taken off for his historic flight. Barrett did this driving the Budweiser Rocket, a branded rocket-powered three-wheel vehicle, and wearing a Rolex Cosmograph.

OPPOSITE: Malcolm Campbell in his Bluebird car in 1935 when he became the first man to exceed 300mph.

ABOVE: US Air Force test pilot Chuck Yeager in front of the Bell X-1 aircraft in Palmdale, California, in 1953.

Summiting Mount Everest

In the 1930s, Rolex started equipping mountaineering teams on Himalayan expeditions with its watches. It did this to test how the watches would react when exposed to extreme conditions at high altitudes.

As the climbers fed back on how the watches performed, improvements were made to subsequent models. This is a fundamental pillar of Rolex's strategy: to test its watches in real-world situations, or – as it describes it – in the 'living laboratory'.

While many had tried, no climber had succeeded in reaching the summit of the Himalaya's Mount Everest until New Zealand beekeeper Edmund Hillary and Tibetan climber Tenzing Norgay in 1953. They were the first people to reach the summit of the world's highest mountain at 8,848 metres (29,028 ft).

The pair were part of a British climbing expedition led by British Army officer Sir John Hunt. Only two men made it to the top, but there was a larger team of 16 climbers supported by hundreds of porters carrying supplies and equipment. Some of the other climbers on the expedition, including Sir Hunt, were equipped with Rolex Oyster Perpetual watches.

Hunt reported back on the performance of the watches, noting how the Perpetual movement proved useful. As the watches did not require winding, climbers were not required to remove their gloves and fiddle with crowns in freezing temperatures. He also noted that the accuracy allowed the team to synchronise effectively, and that they had "come to look upon Rolex Oysters as an important part of high climbing equipment".

Based on feedback from this historic expedition, Rolex launched the Explorer model that same year, which offered increased dial visibility in extreme conditions.

ABOVE: The cover of an Everest colour supplement published by The Times in 1953, showing Sir Edmund Hillary and Tenzing Norgay on the summit of Everest.

Record-breaking Commercial Flights

The 1950s was commercial air travel's golden age, and Rolex went along for the ride. In 1954, the watchmaker developed a tool watch for Pan American airline pilots that was released commercially the following year as the GMT-Master.

Rolex became the official watch brand of the now-defunct airline known affectionately as Pan Am. When Pan Am set out on an ambitious plan in 1959 to complete the first non-stop commercial flight between New York and Moscow, the GMT-Master was in the cockpit on the wrist of Captain Clarence Warren Jr for the 11-hour 25-minute flight.

GMT-Master watches were also worn by the French and British pilots who flew the test flights in 1969 for Concorde, the first supersonic passenger airline.

LEFT: A Pan Am seatbelt and Boeing 707 emergency instructions brochure from the 1970s.

Mariana Trench Dives

In 1960, Lieutenant Don Walsh and Jacques Piccard descended to the bottom of the Mariana Trench, the deepest known depression on Earth at 10,916 metres (37,800 ft) below the surface. They took with them an unusual passenger: a Rolex watch.

Rather than wear the watch, they attached an experimental timepiece called the Rolex Deep Sea Special to the outside of their bathyscaphe vessel. Rolex requested this so it could discover whether the watch would survive the pressure of the deep. It did.

The next diver to successfully descend to the bottom of the Mariana Trench was James Cameron, director of fantasy film *Avatar*, who completed a solo dive in 2012. Rolex created a new experimental watch for this feat. The Deepsea Challenge was attached to the arm of the submersible and successfully withstood 17 tonnes of pressure without cracking.

ABOVE: Filmmaker and record-breaking diver James Cameron wearing a Rolex Submariner.

Pioneering Innovations

Rolex started out as a pioneer. First it foresaw the potential of the wristwatch over the pocket watch. Then it conceived the idea of a case that was waterproof and dustproof, boosting watches' durability. Next came the perpetual movement that put an end to the tedious daily task of winding your watch.

This spirit of innovation has never stopped. The watchmaker is constantly seeking out new ideas, many of which have shaped the entire watch industry, and elevating popular watch features by adding its own spin to them.

From being the first watchmaker to add a date window to the dial, to developing a watch that can travel to the bottom of the sea, and inventing new colours of ceramics previously thought impossible, these are just a few of those innovations.

OPPOSITE: A Rolex Submariner, which will remain waterproof at depths of up to 300m.

ABOVE: An Explorer II on a green NATO fabric strap.

The Oyster Perpetual

When Rolex first started out, all watch movements had to be wound by hand to keep them running. Hans Wilsdorf envisioned a future in which this daily chore would be eliminated.

In 1931, Rolex heralded the age of the self-winding watch with the launch of its Oyster Perpetual, fitted with a movement equipped with a perpetual rotor. The calibre harnessed the kinetic energy created by the movement of the watch wearer's arm to power the watch via an oscillating weight. As long as the watch was in motion, it would stay wound. A variation of this Perpetual movement is at the heart of every Rolex watch today.

It is often thought that Rolex was the inventor of the automatic watch, but this is not true. A self-winding wristwatch mechanism was first invented a decade earlier by English watchmaker John Harwood, who it is said got the idea by watching children playing on a seesaw.

Harwood received a Swiss patent for his self-winding wristwatch in 1924 and sold the rights to the movement to watch brand Fortis. Two years later, Fortis launched a line of mass-produced self-winding wristwatches called the Harwood Automatic at the Schweizer Mustermesse Basela watch fair in Basel, Switzerland.

Harwood's invention and Rolex's movement did differ. Harwood used a hammer-winding mechanism while Rolex used a weighted rotor turning through a full circle. Marketing zeal did lead Rolex to claim to have invented the first self-winding wristwatch in 1955, but the brand ran an apology in The Sunday Express newspaper a year later. It also created an ad crediting Harwood for his invention, and paid homage to Abraham-Louis Perrelet who created a self-winding pocket watch in the late 18th century.

ABOVE: An Oyster Perpetual Submariner.

A Date Window

The Oyster Perpetual was a huge success. It was a highly precise wristwatch that was proven to be waterproof and dustproof, and thanks to its perpetual motor it never required winding. So, what was next?

The answer was something that will seem so obvious to watch fans today that it is hard to imagine it once had to be invented: the date window.

With the launch of the Datejust in 1945, Rolex added a new novelty by displaying the date in an aperture on the dial, positioned at 3 o'clock. Prior to this, watches that carried the date had done so by using an additional hand to point to markings on the outer edge of the dial.

Once the date was set on the Datejust, it automatically changed at midnight each night. In 1956, Rolex's watchmakers improved this so that the change became instantaneous. Blink and you'll miss it.

LEFT: A Datejust showing the date window at 3 o'clock.

The Cyclops

The Datejust's date window proved to be hugely popular, and so thoughts at Rolex turned to how it could be improved. The answer was legibility, and the solution was to overlay the window with a magnifying glass to make it easier to read at a glance.

Rolex created a patented lens to perform this function in the early 1950s. It named it Cyclops, after the one-eyed giant from Greek mythology.

When the Cyclops made its debut on a Datejust model in 1953, it was made from plexiglass. It would later be made in sapphire crystal when Rolex upgraded the glass covering its dials to this tougher material in the 1970s. The Cyclops was further enhanced with a double layer of anti-reflective coating.

ABOVE: A 1959 Rolex Oyster Perpetual
watch on a leather strap.

RIGHT: A Rolex
Oyster Perpetual
Datejust with a
Jubilee bracelet.

An Anti-magnetic Watch

Magnetic fields can be a problem for watches, interfering with the working parts of mechanical movements and compromising precision. Rolex sought to create a workaround, with the needs of scientists working in fields such as telecommunications, medical technology, aerospace and electrotechnical industries in mind. It wanted to create a watch these professionals could wear at work without worrying about loss of accuracy or damage due to magnetism.

By 1956, its watchmakers had cracked it. Inserting a magnetic shield made of two ferromagnetic alloys within an Oyster case meant the movement within could resist interference of up to 1,000 gauss (80,000 a/m). At the time, most anti-magnetic watches on the market could only stand up to about 4,800 a/m. The watch was named Milgauss, combining the French *mille* for thousand and gauss, the unit used to measure magnetic induction at that time.

Rolex asked for the Milgauss to be put to the test at CERN, the European organisation for nuclear research in Geneva, which is today home to the Hadron Collider. After stringent testing, the Milgauss passed. It would later become the watch of choice for CERN scientists, who it is said lobbied Rolex to develop the anti-magnetic watch in the first place.

To highlight the antimagnetic alteration to the Oyster case, the caseback of the Milgauss was decorated with a 'B' with an arrow above it, which is the symbol for magnetic flux density.

When the Milgauss was relaunched in 2007, following two decades of non-production, the watch's antimagnetic capabilities were further enhanced by making the oscillator and the escape wheel – key components within the movement – from paramagnetic materials to further limit the chance of interference.

Deep Sea Special Experiment

In the 1950s, Rolex watchmakers began work on an experimental watch that would be capable of travelling to the bottom of the ocean. The challenge was to create a timepiece that wouldn't crack under the intense pressure of the deep, start letting in water or simply stop working.

The watch was called the Deep Sea Special. It was a simple affair in terms of timekeeping, with a small black dial with Rolex branding, hour and minute markers, and three hands. The dial was fixed to a bi-coloured metal bracelet. The defining feature was its thick, bubble-like crystal that covered the dial. This sapphire crystal needed to be much thicker than that of an ordinary watch to withstand the pressure deep beneath the waves.

In 1953, this experimental watch was put to a real-world test. Rolex approached Swiss physicist Auguste Piccard, inventor of the bathyscaphe, a vessel capable of travelling to great depths. Along with his son, Jacques Piccard, Auguste was making a series of dives to explore the ocean floor. Father and son agreed to attach the Deep Sea Special to the exterior of the bathyscaphe when they made their underwater expeditions.

The first voyage successfully took the Deep Sea Special to a depth of 3,150 metres (10,300 ft) in waters off the Pontine Islands in the Tyrrhenian Sea. Much to Rolex's delight, the watch survived in perfect working order.

There would be many more dives, and many more variations of the Deep Sea Special, the design of which was tweaked each time to improve it. In 1960, the watch made its most famous dive with the Piccards, all the way to the bottom of the Mariana Trench, the deepest part of the ocean.

Oystersteel, Everose and Chromalight

Stainless steel is a popular metal of choice within the Rolex offering, due to its durability and accessible pricing. In the 1980s, Rolex upgraded the steel it was using for its diving watches, swapping the industry standard 316L steel for a tougher 904L that was less likely to corrode in salt water.

By 2003, it had started to exclusively produce new watches in this higher grade of steel, which has a dual benefit of acquiring an exceptional sheen when polished. In 2018, Rolex started to brand this material as Oystersteel, reflecting the fact that it was producing its own specific alloy at its foundry in Switzerland.

Rolex has also tinkered with the alloys of its precious metals. In 2005, it introduced Everose, a bespoke blend of 18-carat rose gold, within its Cosmograph Daytona line. Everose has a distinctive soft pink hue that is created through a mix of pure gold, copper, silver and platinum. In its patent application for the metal, Rolex claimed that the addition of this final metal would protect its rose gold from the fading that can sometimes occur with other less luxurious blends.

Another material to have a rebrand thanks to Rolex's growing in-house capabilities was the coating it uses to make its watch dials glow in the dark. In 2008, it announced it would stop using watchmaking's favourite Super-LumiNova coating in favour of its own Chromalight that glows blue rather than green and lasts longer, according to the watchmaker.

PREVIOUS: A dupliccte of the Deep Sea Special that travelled to the bottom of the Mariana Trench.

RIGHT: A bi-colour Datejust in Oystersteel and yellow gold.

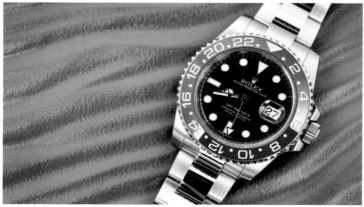

Cerachrom

Ceramic has been used in watchmaking since the 1980s but by the early Noughties it exploded, driven by the popularity of Chanel's J12 watches. During this time, Rolex was conducting experiments with ceramic and in 2005 it unveiled its own offering – Cerachrom.

Ceramic is virtually scratchproof and its colour is unaffected by ultraviolet rays, so Rolex used Cerachrom to add colour to the bezels of its professional watches. The first watch to be updated with a Cerechrom bezel was a GMT-Master II. To ensure legibility of the 24-hour graduations on the bezel, the engraved markings were coated with a thin layer of platinum.

In 2013, Rolex revealed a technological leap forward in ceramics by producing Cerachrom bezels in dual colours. Rather than fusing two different colours of ceramic together, it applied separate colours to a single ceramic insert – an incredibly difficult technical feat that Rolex claims was a world first. The first example of this was a GMT-Master II with a blue and black bezel that fans would later nickname the 'Batman'. A red and blue version released in 2014 would become the 'Pepsi'.

Rolex was also a pioneer when it came to the shades of colours it managed to achieve. Red ceramic, for example, was originally thought to be impossible as it was believed there were no pigments stable enough to endure the manufacturing process. Rolex got around this by using alumina, a mineral oxide used to create synthetic rubies.

OPPOSITE TOP: A close-up of the green Cerachrom bezel of a Submariner.

OPPOSITE BOTTOM: A GMT-Master II 'Batman' with blue and black Cerachrom bezel.

Oysterflex

With a new line of Yacht-Master watches released in 2015 came a new strap option: the Oysterflex. This sportier option was a black elastomer strap, but unlike other rubber straps on the market, it had a hidden superpower. Within the strap was concealed a flexible blade made of titanium and nickel, which improved its durability.

The shape of the strap was also carefully considered. Rather than lying flat against the wrist, it has a raised centre, and underneath this are wing-like formations. These help air to circulate and reduce perspiration, as well as acting as stabilisers to centre the watch. It also has a Rolex Glidelock system that allows for the length of the strap to be adjusted by 15mm without the need for tools.

The Oysterflex is now available on a number of Rolex models including Sky-Dweller, Cosmograph Daytona and the Yacht-Master watches.

OPPOSITE: A Yachtmaster with Everose gold case and Oysterflex strap.

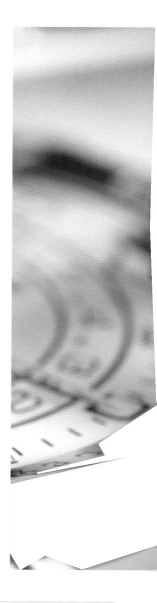

Made in Switzerland

In 1920, Rolex left Britain to relocate to Switzerland, the heartland of watchmaking. The country truly is a paragon of precision and quality, and its connection to watchmaking is deeply ingrained in its culture and commerce. As such, the phase 'Swiss made' carries much weight, instantly conveying the message that the watch bearing such as stamp is a superior product.

Over the past century, Rolex has invested in its watchmaking facilities in Switzerland, driven by a mission to bring as much of the process of creating a watch inhouse as possible. This doesn't just apply to the movements, but all the elements, from the dials to the bracelets. In recent years, it has also focused on creating its own raw materials such as gold and ceramic.

LEFT: Rolex branding atop a building on the edge of Geneva's Lac Léman in Switzerland.

The Manufacture

Switzerland is famous for its watchmaking industry, and Rolex is right at the heart of it. The brand creates all of its watches there, and has dedicated itself to a strategy of bringing as much of the processes in house as possible to make it a truly integrated manufacture. Across four core sites, 9,000 employees are engaged in the production, marketing and sale of an estimated 1 million watches each year.

In the central Acacias district of Geneva, you will find the Rolex global headquarters. This is where the brand's top executives work, and those focused on the business side of the brand: commercial activities, communications, sponsorship, philanthropy, exports and after-sales service. Some production also takes place here, including the final assembly and testing of the watches.

Four kilometres away in the Plan-les-Ouates district, you will find another Rolex facility. This site, which is comprised of six 65-metre-long wings linked by a central corridor, was opened in 2005. Here, all production activities relating to the creation of its watch cases and bracelets take place. Plan-les-Ouates is also home to the Rolex foundry, where it produces its bespoke metal alloys, such as Everose, Oystersteel and RLX Titanium.

Creating cases and bracelets can be a laborious task. An Oyster case has up to 20 components and can require as many as 300 manufacturing stages, while a bracelet can consist of 190 components, all of which are put together by hand.

BELOW: The Rolex headquarters in Geneva, Switzerland.

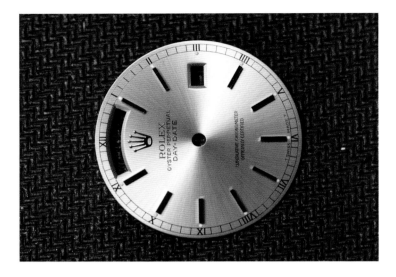

On the other side of town is Chêne-Bourg, home to Rolex's dial makers and gem setters. A dial might seem like one of the simpler components in horology, but the a Rolex dial must go through 60 processes to make it ready for insertion into a timepiece. This covers the creation of the dial itself, whether in brass or 18-carat gold, as well as that of the appliques, such as hour markers, diamond details and that famous Rolex branding.

Much of the colour you see on Rolex watches is introduced at Chêne-Bourg through techniques such as PVD (Physical Vapour Deposition) and lacquer work. It is here Rolex mixes up its patented Cerachrom ceramic and applies its Chromalight glow-in-the-dark Super-LumiNova coatings. It is also where its gemmologists work, meticulously assessing the quality of diamonds and coloured gemstones before approving them for use by the watchmaker's gem setters.

About 150 kilometres north of Geneva, at the foot of the Jura mountains, is Bienne, another Swiss town that is famous for its links to watchmaking. This is where Rolex produces its movements, manufacturing the 200 to 400 components required to make a single calibre, and then assembling them by hand.

Demand for Rolex watches is at an all-time high, and to keep up with production, the watchmaker is constantly expanding is facilities. Both the Acacias and Bienne sites were extended in 2022, and the brand will open new production facilities in Fribourg, western Switzerland. It has committed 1 billion Swiss francs to building a major new production site in the town of Bulle that should deliver its first timepieces in 2029. As an interim measure, it is also opening temporary production facilities in Romont and Villaz-Saint-Pierre that will start producing watches by 2025.

OPPOSITE: A golden dial taken from a Rolex 1800 series Day-Date.

LEFT: A lens magnifies a Roman numeral hour marker on a Cellini dial.

The Watchmakers

At Rolex's facilities in Geneva, there are thousands of watchmakers, all dressed in white lab coats, working silently in pristine environments. Each will have their own speciality, and will use a blend of old and new knowledge to do their part in the creation of a Rolex. That could be building a movement, perfecting a dial, or experimenting with prototypes in the research and development division.

To be a Rolex watchmaker requires continual learning. Those who don the white coats and loupes must be up to date with all the latest models, calibres and techniques. To facilitate this career-long attitude to learning, Rolex opened its Training Centre in Geneva in 2018. The 4,300 square metre Training Centre comprises 20 spaces, each equipped with cutting-edge educational tools.

Training modules delivered include lessons on the company's history, culture and values, as well as more practical

LEFT: There are Rolex-accredited watchmakers all over the world.

watchmaking courses. Each year, about 100 apprentices, 100 interns and 3,000 employees take part in some form of training there.

Rolex is dedicated to bringing up the next generation of watchmakers. In 1984, it became the first watch manufacturer to take on apprentices, and since then it has trained hundreds of aspiring watchmakers of different ages and backgrounds in one of 15 trades available within its wheelhouse. Today, there are more than 170 teenagers and young adults within its apprenticeship programmes in Bienne and Geneva.

It has also sought to spread the Rolex know-how far beyond Switzerland. There are Rolex training centres across the world, which are used to train local watchmakers so they can work for the brand or for local Rolex-accredited dealers. Rather than building new watches, these trained watchmakers will offer servicing and repairs.

A shortage of watchmakers is a common problem across the industry, with many skilled watchmakers retiring and not being replaced, creating a skills gap. This was caused in part by the arrival of battery-powered quartz watch movements in the 1980s, which led to a decline in traditional watchmaking and watchmakers. The mechanical watch revival of the past two decades has led to an increase in ownership and production, meaning more watchmakers are required. Training schemes such as Rolex's are trying to catch up.

In the US, for example, the number of watchmakers fell from about 32,000 to 6,500 between 1973 and 2000. To address this, Rolex funds the Lititz Watch Technicum watchmaking school, which opened in Lititz, Pennsylvania, in 2001 and provides free training to a select few each year. It has so far produced more than 150 qualified watchmakers.

Movements

The movement, or calibre, of a watch is the mechanism inside the case that keeps it in working order. This complex architecture of cogs, wheels and springs not only delivers precision timekeeping but can be tweaked to introduce additional functions such as a date window or chronograph timing.

Many watchmakers outsource this complicated job to expert movement makers, such as the much-favoured ETA manufacturer owned by Swatch Group. Rolex has worked with a number of manufacturers, including Valjoux, but it is Aegler, the company it first turned to for small movements back in its Wilsdorf & Davis days, that it has worked most closely with.

The first Rolex movement Aegler produced was the ground-breaking self-winding calibre 620 for the Oyster Perpetual, which launched in 1931. In 1936, it unveiled two new movements: calibre 520 allowed the seconds to be displayed in a sub dial at 6 o'clock, referred to as small seconds; calibre 530 introduced a sweeping seconds hand that moved continuously round the dial in a smooth movement that has become an iconic feature of Rolex watches.

Rolex and Aegler created many movements together. Some have suggested there might have been as many as 100 iterations; each time, Rolex asked for its own branding to be present on the mechanism to create a sense of ownership. In 2004, Rolex bought Aegler and incorporated it into the business, allowing the brand to finally be able to say that it makes its movements in house.

The following year, it introduced two major developments

to protect the accuracy of its movements. These were a blue Parachrom hairspring made from an anti-magnetic alloy of niobium, zirconium and oxygen, and the Paraflex shock absorber.

Tribology

ABOVE: The precision of a watch relies on every moving part within the movement.

A Rolex watch will tick 250 million times a year, and each tick is created by a complex system of gears and cogs. To ensure these components work to their fullest potential, the watchmaker has a team of tribologists.

These experts combine the skillsets of engineers, chemists and watchmakers to apply lubrication to the watches' moving parts. It is a delicate skill: too much and you'll slow it down, too little and it will seize up. They also assess external components, such as bracelets. Rolex creates its own lubricants in house, with each having required about a decade of research and development to bring to fruition.

Rather than just creating solutions to problems, Rolex tribologists are now involved in the design of the watches so they can anticipate and avert issues. A good example of this is the ceramic inserts found in the President bracelets that reduce wear and tear; an idea brought by a tribologist.

The Foundry

Rolex has come a long way since its beginnings in London selling other watchmakers' work. Now, as well as producing its own watches and movements, it is also committed to developing its own raw materials.

Perhaps the most famous of these is Oystersteel. Rolex started using a bespoke blend of 904L steel in 1985, although it didn't introduce the brand name until 2018. This particular type was selected from more than 3,500 grades of industrial steel, chosen for its ability to retain its brilliance no matter what conditions it is exposed to.

Oystersteel is rich in chromium and molybdenum, which makes it particularly resistant to impact and corrosion. Nothing is left to chance, however. Throughout the creation process, Rolex's metallurgists control and refine its microstructure before machining it in a way that further strengthens it. It is then the job of Rolex's polishers to create that signature Oystersteel shine.

Rolex also uses its foundry to make its own gold. In 2005, it created Everose, the brand's take on 18-carat rose gold. Again, the alloy was manipulated to create a superior metal that offered increased radiance and strength. The exact formula remains a closely guarded secret, but it does contain 75% gold, 20% copper, platinum, palladium and indium.

In 2022, Rolex introduced another proprietary metal – RLX titanium. This metal is favoured by watchmakers due to its strength and lightness. It is denser than aluminium but lighter than steel. Offering this grade 5 titanium required more than simply whipping up a new alloy. As titanium is so difficult to work with, the watchmaker had to develop new in-house techniques that were capable of processing it, including dedicated polishing techniques.

ABOVE: An 18-carat gold Datejust on a Jubilee bracelet.

LEFT: Until 1974, 14-carat gold was the purest gold that could be sold in the US, so many early 20th century Rolexes were made in this alloy rather than the standard 18-carat gold.

The Bracelets

Rolex first introduced metal bracelets in the 1930s, collaborating with Gay Frères, a maker of renown that produced for many other brands, including Audemars Piguet and Zenith. Rolex would eventually buy the Gay Frères business in 1998, as part of its strategy to bring all of its manufacturing in house.

As the popularity of this new type of strap rose, Rolex sought to create something special and in 1947 it submitted a patent for what would become the Oyster bracelet. The iconic three-link bracelet is known for its durability and comfort, and comes as standard on many models.

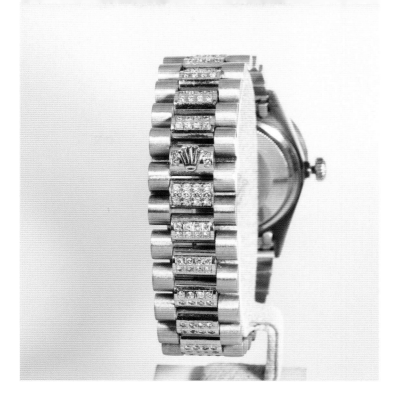

Other bracelet styles to have joined the Rolex family over the years have included the five-link Jubilee, introduced in 1945 on the Datejust, the rounded three-link gold or platinum President bracelet only available on Day-Date models, and the sleek Pearlmaster bracelet for the line of the same name that was discontinued in 2022. In 2014, Rolex also introduced its flexible Oysterflex elastomer strap that has extra strength due to two titanium-nickel blades hidden within.

OPPOSITE: A Rolex Jubilee five-link bracelet in steel and gold.

TOP: A Rolex President bracelet with diamonds set into the links.

Gemmology

Rolex makes a relatively small number of gem-set watches each year, but when it does roll out the diamonds, there is a team of gemmologists and setters at its Chêne-Bourg facility ready to handle them.

Even though the diamonds set into a Rolex watch are tiny – it takes 3,000 stones to completely cover a dial using the snow-setting method – each one must be certified as being internally flawless and at the top end of the colour scale (D to G).

Rolex has also experimented with coloured gemstones, famously adding multi-coloured sapphires to the dial and bezel of its Rainbow Cosmograph in 2012 and following up with a Rainbow Daytona. It also creates watches with hardstone dials, using slices of semi-precious gems such as turquoise, sodalite and chrysoprase in place of the usual brass. This flourish was first introduced in the 1970s in partnership with celebrated dial maker Stern Frères, now renamed Stern Création.

LEFT: American rapper Macklemore wears a fully diamond-set Rolex Day-Date.

Colour Coding

When a designer selects a new colour for a Rolex dial, they first must consult one of the brand's scientists, who will deduce the method of creation. This will be followed by three months of research and trials; sometimes, it can take years for the perfect colour to be achieved.

The different techniques that Rolex watchmakers use to add colour include lacquer, which is often used for black or white dials, and Cerachrom ceramic inserts on bezels. Electroplating is used for dials with a metallic finish. Silver can be electroplated onto a dial to create a sunray effect, or a complex blend of metals can be electroplated to create champagne-coloured dials.

An application that has grown in popularity in watches is PVD (Physical Vapour Deposition) coatings. This method of adding very thin layers of colour by injecting ceramic powder into a high-power plasma flame under a vacuum was first developed by NASA. Rolex watchmakers will apply this multi-tonal precise colouring within vacuum chambers that mimic the pressure of outer space.

Certain colours have made Rolex watches very collectible, such as the green 'Hulk' Submariner. One collectible dial colour was actually the result of a production snafu: sought-after 'tropical' dials are found on watches from the 1950s and 1960s that once had black glossy dials but have since turned brown over time. They are so named because exposure to UV rays caused the colour change, and many early examples came from hotter climes.

RIGHT: A gold Day-Date with green dial and matching green strap.

Testing

If you have ever owned a Rolex, or even just researched the brand, you will be familiar with the phrase 'superlative chronometer'. The concept first emerged in the 1950s and refers to the testing a watch must undergo to meet the brand's exacting standards.

All Rolex watches are Superlative Chronometers, and you will see this printed on the dials. The testing is carried out in house and guarantees a precision of -2/+2 seconds per day (meaning the watch will lose or gain no more than two seconds each day). The Superlative Chronometer certification, which was updated in 2015, also ensures that a watch is waterproof.

Before undergoing this testing, loose Rolex movements are first submitted to COSC (the Swiss Official Chronometer Testing Institute) for certification. To pass the COSC testing, the movements must have an accuracy of -4/+6 seconds per day – far less stringent that Rolex's Superlative Chronometer standards.

When it comes to testing the waterproofness of a Rolex, the brand first subjects the watch to an air pressure test. Once passed, the timepiece will progress to a 1.3 tonne stainless steel tank in Rolex's Les Acacias factory in Geneva. This is a hyperbaric pressure chamber created by French maritime engineering specialists Comex, for which Rolex made watches in the 1960s. The tank is filled with water, then the pressure is increased 25% beyond that which would be experienced at the depth the watch is supposed to be waterproof to.

LEFT: A Cosmograph with Superlative Chronometer branding on the dial.

The Icons

How well do you know the Rolex family of watches? Can you pick out an Explorer from an Explorer II? Do you know the depth to which a Deepsea model can dive? Each watch collection embodies part of the Rolex story, and also charts the history of watchmaking itself. We can divine the innovations, trends and interests of the times through the watches that the brand produced.

In this chapter, we look at Rolex's most iconic models, from the Oyster Perpetual to the Perpetual 1908 line of dress watches. Discover the origin stories of the models you admire, find out how to identify them, and learn what it is that sets them apart. Your deep dive into Rolex icons starts now.

RIGHT: A Rolex Submariner with black Cerachrom bezel.

Oyster Perpetual

The classic Rolex is the Oyster Perpetual, making it an ideal choice for purists. This elegant design is a direct descendant of the original 1926 Oyster, which was one of the world's first waterproof wristwatches.

The Oyster Perpetual launched in 1945 and was so named as it combined the robust, watertight Oyster case with the watchmaker's Perpetual movement. This calibre capitalises on the movement of the wearer to influence an oscillating weight that automatically winds the watch, keeping it ticking.

Today's Oyster Perpetual case is crafted from a single block of Oystersteel. The watch has myriad dial colour options and is fitted with a three-link Oyster bracelet. On the dial, you will find a minimalist display of raised hour markers and a minutes/seconds track around the outer edge. Time is kept by three sleek hands, and good legibility is guaranteed by the application of an anti-reflective coating to the sapphire crystal that covers the dial.

The Oyster Perpetual is waterproof up to a depth of 100m. Its fluted caseback is hermetically sealed using a tool that only Rolex watchmakers have access to; protecting it against unauthorised tampering that could jeopardise its impermeable seal. The winding crown has been fitted with the brand's Twinlock double waterproofing system to ensure it screws down securely against the case, just like the watertight hatch of a submarine.

LEFT: A steel Oyster
Perpetual with teal dial.

It is often the first watch a Rolex collector will buy due to its timeless good looks and its status as the most accessibly priced Rolex. However, later versions of the Oyster 41 have been made with solid 18-carat gold hands and hour markers, proving that the appeal of this model goes far beyond its affordability.

Datejust

Displaying the date on the dial of a watch might seem obvious today, but in 1945 when the Datejust made its debut, it was revolutionary. On its release, the Datejust became the first self-winding waterproof chronometer wristwatch to display the date in a window, positioned at 3 o'clock on the dial.

When the watch was first presented on Rolex's 40th anniversary, founder Hans Wilsdorf said: "This is the pinnacle of watchmaking science. It encapsulates every discovery made to date." He was referring to the timepiece's chronometric precision, waterproofness, self-winding Perpetual movement, and then the date window.

Up until that point, wristwatches that displayed the date did so via a hand on the dial that would point to markers placed at its edge. The Datejust instead used a rotating disc positioned beneath the dial that would show the correct date via an aperture.

In 1953, this marvel of horology became even more prominent on the dial with the invention of the Cyclops. It was a section of magnifying glass built into the crystal covering the dial, not unlike bi-focal lenses in spectacles; wearers no longer had to squint to read the date on their wrists. In 1956, the transition from one date to the next became instantaneous, jumping forward at the stroke of midnight.

Due to pioneering engineering balanced with a classic design, the Datejust became a favourite watch among many notable men. Winston Churchill, Dwight D. Eisenhower and Martin Luther King all wore one.

There have been many variations of the Datejust throughout the years. In 2009, Rolex launched the Datejust II, a line of models with a 41mm case designed to cater to the vogue at that time for large watches. This was discontinued in 2016.

Air-King

The Air-King is a celebration of Rolex's links with aviation. The earliest models were made for the British Royal Air Force as part of a series of watches called Air, during and immediately after World War II. The King element of the name refers to the original 34mm case, which at that time was considered large, although it would be modest by today's standards.

When the Air-King launched to the public in 1945 it looked not too dissimilar to the traditional Oyster models, with a cream dial and Arabic numerals. In the 1950s, it started to take on its own aesthetic, swapping a leather strap for a steel bracelet and numerals for hour markers. A bespoke Air-King font was developed to be used on the dial.

An intriguing moment in the history of the Air-King was when Rolex briefly allowed corporations to customise its watch dials. The most famous of these is the highly collectible Domino's Pizza Air-King, with the pizzeria's red-and-blue logo stamped on the dial. It was made during the 1970s and 1980s to be gifted to store managers hitting weekly sales of more than $20,000 four weeks in a row. The sales challenge remains ongoing, although Domino's managers are now rewarded with an Oyster Perpetual that has more subtle branding on the case and bracelet rather than on the dial.

Contemporary Air-King watches cut a striking figure with a signature black dial lit up by bright green on the Rolex logo and seconds hand. The large, white numerals are designed for ease of reading by aviators, and that iconic Air-King font remains unchanged since the 1950s.

LEFT: An Air-King model with blue dial and Oyster bracelet.

PREVIOUS: A steel Datejust on a five-link Jubilee bracelet.

Explorer and Explorer II

The Rolex Explorer was created for adventure. As such, it has been put to the test in some of the most extreme reaches of the planet, on the wrists of polar explorers, mountaineers and cavers.

The watch was first launched in 1953 and its design was based

on feedback given to the brand by real-life adventurers. One of the most important requirements was that it should be legible in any condition. In response to this, the Explorer was fitted with a black dial and brightly contrasting, large white hour markers with numerals at 3 o'clock, 6 o'clock and 9 o'clock. Those markers are coated with Chromalight, a luminescent material that emits a lasting blue glow in low light, allowing it to be read in the dark.

The original Explorer was followed in 1976 with the Explorer II; both models are still in production today. The Explorer II differed in a number of ways, including having a sportier design that took it further away from the classic Oyster silhouette.

This second model also has increased functionality that is, again, designed due to the likelihood that it will be put to the test in extremes. As well as introducing a date window, it also has a bright-orange hand tipped with an arrow. This tracks a number ring on the bezel of the watch. It can be used to keep track of a second time zone, or to act as a 24-hour clock so that explorers know whether it is night or day. The latter use has made it a popular choice for scientists, explorers and athletes who spend time in dark caves or underground, as well as those exposed to either constant darkness or ceaseless light in the Arctic or Antarctica.

LEFT: An Explorer II with white 'Polar' dial.

Submariner

The Submariner is a watch made for divers. When it was first released in 1953, it was one of the first of its kind: a watch made to be worn and put to work underwater. Following on from the creation of the Oyster – the world's first waterproof watch – the Submariner became the first watch to be waterproof to a depth of 100 meters (330ft). This was a major breakthrough in watchmaking and set a benchmark for diver's watches. Over the decades, of course, that benchmark has shifted. Today, Submariners can go three times deeper than the original, being waterproof up to 300 meters (1,000ft).

Every element of these watches links back to the activity they were designed for: diving. To ensure the watches are legible underwater, where the light is often low, Submariners have a black dial with bold hour markers and wide hands, all coated in the brand's luminescent Chromalight to make them glow in the dark. A date window with Cyclops magnifier is an optional extra that was first introduced in 1969.

Today's Submariners have an Oyster bracelet fitted with an Oysterlock safety clasp to protect against accidental opening while underwater. A Glidelock extension system allows the bracelet to be adjusted without tools, so it can easily be fitted over a diving suit.

One of the most important elements of this watch is its unidirectional bezel. The scratch-proof ceramic insert is engraved with a 60-minute graduation that allows divers to monitor their diving time and decompression stops. The knurled edges of the bezel allow for good grip. This functionality makes it a vital tool for staying safe underwater.

GMT-Master II

The GMT-Master II is the watch of choice for global travellers, as it can be used to simultaneously tell the time in two different time zones. The hour, minute and seconds hands tell the time on the dial in a primary zone, as on a regular watch. A longer red hand tipped with an arrow can be used to keep track of a second time zone by pointing to numbers on the bezel representing the 24-hour clock. This second time zone is set by twisting the bezel to the correct number of hours between it and the original time zone.

The first of these watches, named simply GMT-Master, was created in 1955 as a professional tool for airline pilots. Both French and British pilots testing the supersonic Concorde planes wore one, and the GMT-Master also became the official watch of American airline Pan America, known as Pan Am.

In 1982, the GMT-Master transitioned to the GMT-Master II after a new movement was created that allowed the hour hand on the watch to be changed independently to the other hands, speeding up the processes. The name change differentiates between models with the older functionality and the new.

Many GMT-Master IIs have a bi-coloured bezel, with the colours switching over at 6- and 18-hour markers on the bezel. This helps travellers to know at a glance whether their second time zone is in day or night.

LEFT: A GMT-Master II with 'Batman' bezel and Jubilee bracelet.

PREVIOUS: A black-dial Submariner on a steel Oyster bracelet.

The earliest 24-hour bezels were made of plexiglass. This was then upgraded to anodised aluminium in 1959 and high-tech ceramic in 2005. The original bezel colour combination was blue and red, which is nicknamed 'Pepsi' by watch aficionados, but there have been many variations over the decades.

Day-Date

The Day-Date is perhaps the most prestigious of all the Rolex models. It has even been given the nickname the 'President' due to the number of US presidents who have worn one; John F. Kennedy had one, as did Lyndon Johnson, Dwight Eisenhower and Gerald Ford.

The Day-Date was released in 1956, and brought with it a new watchmaking complication. While the Datejust added the date of the month to the dial, the Day-Date built on that again with the addition of a window displaying the name of the day. Both the day and the date automatically click forward at midnight; a pleasingly fleeting transformation for night-owl Rolex wearers to try to catch.

The day, which is displayed in a window located at 12 o'clock, can be customised to the wearer's language. Rolex offers Day-Dates in 26 languages, using the Latin, Arabic, Cyrillic, Hebrew, Japanese and Chinese alphabets, as well as Ge'ez, an alphasyllabary used in the Horn of Africa.

What makes this watch so coveted as a status symbol by powerful people, other than its iconic design and long list of famous owners, is its prohibitive price tag. The Day-Date is only produced in solid 18-carat gold or platinum, making it a luxurious purchase.

Some early Day-Date models were sold on a leather strap with a gold buckle, but modern versions are fitted with a President bracelet. This style of precious metal bracelet was launched by Rolex in the same year as the Day-Date. Crafted in solid gold or platinum, it has a distinctive look with three strips of semi-circular links. Hidden within the links are ceramic inserts that enhance the bracelet's flexibility and longevity.

ABOVE: A gold Day-Date with diamond hour markers on a graduated green dial.

Milgauss

The Milgauss is Rolex's pioneering anti-magnetic watch. It was created in 1956 to withstand interference of up to 1,000 gauss, which is where the name comes from – a combination of the French word *mille* for thousand and gauss for the unit of measurement.

This technical innovation was created with the scientific community in mind. At that time, scientists working with magnetic fields could not wear a watch – or use one for calculations – due to concerns over a loss of precision caused by magnetism interfering with the movement. Rolex combatted this by inserting a magnetic shield made of two ferromagnetic alloys within the Oyster case to protect the movement within.

One of the most striking design elements of the original Milgauss watch was its lightning bolt-shaped seconds hand. Rolex swapped this out in the 1960s for a standard hand when it introduced a smooth bezel in place of the original rotating bezel; something that watch experts credit with a decline in the model's popularity at that time.

The Milgauss was discontinued in 1988, but would make a comeback nearly two decades later when it was relaunched in 2007. The timing of this reboot coincided with the turning on the following year of the Hadron Collider at CERN, the European organisation for nuclear research in Geneva where the Milgauss was sent for testing in the 1950s.

LEFT: A Milgauss with a white dial decorated with orange hour markers and a lightning bolt seconds hand.

As well as boasting improved anti-magnetic functionality, this new generation of Milgauss had a fresh design that stood out. The lightning bolt hand was back, now coloured bright orange, and some of the models had a green sapphire crystal over bold blue dials.

In 2023, the Milgauss was once again retired, with Rolex announcing it would cease production.

Lady-Datejust

Rolex had created watches for women since the earliest days of the brand with dress watches, such as the Rolex Queen. Indeed, the watchmaker's first official ambassador, Mercedes Gleitze, was female. The athlete wore an Oyster watch around her neck during a historic swim across the English Channel in 1927. This inspired an ad campaign promoting the "amphibious Oyster" as a "heatproof, waterproof, dustproof, coldproof, perspirationproof" timepiece for active women at work and play.

It wasn't until 1957, however, that the brand produced a tool watch designed specifically for women: the Lady-Datejust. This was essentially just a smaller version of the popular Datejust. However, the downsizing to fit women's wrists proved to be a horological challenge, as the entire movement within the watch had to be resized. At its smallest, the Lady-DateJust had a case size of just 26mm, but modern versions start at 28mm.

Therefore, what might have seemed like a simple shift was actually quite complex. As Rolex founder Hans Wilsdorf said at the time: "Ladies want the best of both worlds: a tiny watch and an accurate movement. Yet, the smaller the watch, the more difficult it is to make it accurate."

The Lady-Datejust is a certified superlative chronometer, like all Rolex watches, setting it apart in the women's watch market, which is so often dominated by diamond-set quartz models that value style over substance.

Style is important too, of course. Over the years, the Lady-Datejust family has swelled with a growing number of variations. These include diamonds on the bezel or as hour markers, solid gold versions, mother-of-pearl dials in place of steel and, as of 2021, gold timepieces completely covered, from dial and case to bracelet, with pavé diamonds.

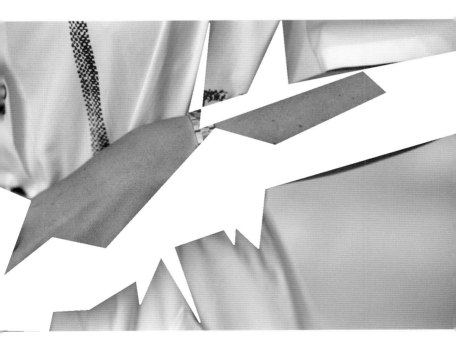

Cosmograph Daytona

The Cosmograph Daytona is Rolex's motorsports-inspired chronograph. A chronograph is a style of watch used for precision timing in sports, with a stopwatch functionality controlled by pushers either side of the crown. Race times are measured in three sub dials on the watch that track seconds, minutes and hours.

Rolex had been producing chronographs since the 1920s, long before the arrival of the Cosmograph Daytona. In 1940, it created its first split-seconds chronograph that allowed

for the timing of two events that start at the same time but finish separately – such as staggered races.

In 1963, Rolex ditched the use of the word chronograph in favour of Cosmograph. This celestial wordplay is thought to have come from Rolex's bid to make the timepiece the official watch of NASA; it lost out to the Omega Speedmaster, which would later be renamed the Speedmaster Moonwatch in recognition of the coup. 'Daytona' was added to the dial of the Cosmograph a year later in recognition of Rolex's sponsorship of the 24 Hours of Daytona automobile race in Florida, which is now known as Rolex 24 at Daytona.

Along with the name change to Cosmograph Daytona came a new innovation. The tachymeter scale, which is used to read average speed over a given distance based on elapsed time, was moved from the edge of the dial to the bezel. Doing so made it more legible and created a style icon coveted by motorsports fans. Perhaps the most famous of these was actor Paul Newman, whose association with the timepiece led to some versions of it (Refs. 6239, 6241, 6262, 6263, 6264 and 6265 that have three-colour dials, Art Deco fonts and a certain style of sub dials) unofficially being branded as Paul Newman Daytonas.

LEFT: Cosmograph Daytona chronograph on an Oyster bracelet.

PREVIOUS: A gold and steel Lady-Datejust with Roman numeral hour markers.

Sea-Dweller, Deepsea and Deepsea Challenge

In 1967, Rolex revealed a new timepiece that would – quite literally – deepen its connection to the oceans. The Sea-Dweller was a professional divers' watch that would remain waterproof at depths of up to 610 meters (2,000ft). This was increased to 1,220 meters (4,000ft) in updated models from 1978.

The Sea-Dweller also addressed a problem many divers using hyperbaric chambers to decompress faced when it came to their watches. During a dive, helium molecules can get trapped in the waterproof case, and during decompression they will then try to escape through a watch's weakest point. This can lead to damage, such as the shattering of a watch's crystal. Rolex's workaround was a patented one-way gas escape valve that allowed the helium to be released safely at a given pressure during decompression, without compromising the waterproofness of the case.

Sea-Dweller models also have a 60-minute graduated unidirectional rotatable bezel in scratch- and corrosion-proof Cerachrom ceramic. This can be used to monitor dive and decompression times, making it a useful tool for divers.

Rolex continued to build on this professional diving legacy with the release of the Deepsea in 2008, which can dive even further, remaining waterproof to depths of 3,900 meters (12,800ft). To withstand the pressure experienced at such depths, the case of this new model had to be redesigned with a Ring Lock System. It uses a nitrogen-alloyed steel ring to support the extra-thick sapphire crystal covering the watch face.

Even more extreme was 2022's Deepsea Challenge watch

that boasts waterproofness up to 11,000 meters (36,090 ft). It is also Rolex's first titanium timepiece – the metal was chosen as it is 40% lighter than steel.

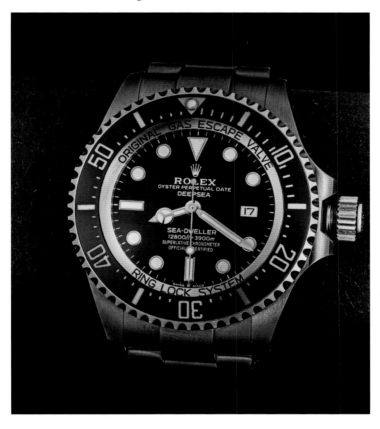

ABOVE: A Deepsea Sea-Dweller diver's watch with Ring Lock System.

OVERLEAF: A Yacht-Master II with its distinctive blue, white and red dial.

Yacht-Master and Yacht-Master II

Rolex released the Yacht-Master in 1992 as a watch for those who like to work and play on the open seas. The watch is a blend of luxury and function, with the bezel perhaps being the best symbol for this. It is crafted in precious metal, often inlaid with a colourful ceramic insert, and accented with 60-minute graduations that allow its wearer to measure time intervals.

While the Yacht-Master is available on an Oyster bracelet, the more practical choice for those expecting the splash of waves is an Oysterflex strap. This rubber-like strap is just as robust as Rolex's bracelets, thanks to a metal blade at the centre of the elastomer, but some believe it offers more comfort.

The Yacht-Master series was expanded and improved in 2007 with the launch of the Yacht-Master II. This watch

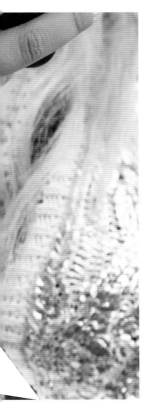

has an instantly recognisable nautical style with its distinctive red, blue and white dial. It also offered up a new complication with the addition of a high-precision chronograph, which will appeal to those who enjoy open-water racing.

Unlike regular chronographs, which count seconds, minutes and hours on separate sub dials, much in the way a stopwatch might, the Yacht-Master II has been tailored to the needs of regatta racing. As such, its main function is to count down. This is because at the start of regatta races, sailors will synchronise their watches in line with flag signals so they know precisely when the race will start. Usually this is a five-minute countdown, but it can be as much as 10 minutes, which is why the programmable countdown arc on the Yacht-Master II dial goes up to 10. It also has a single sub dial for measuring those all-important seconds.

Sky-Dweller

When the Sky-Dweller arrived in 2012 it was the first entirely new Rolex model to launch in two decades. Its function? To act as a companion for world travellers by displaying two time zones simultaneously.

Dual time zone was a complication already available in Rolex's GMT-Master II and Explorer II models, but the Sky-Dweller brought something different. It also had an annual calendar that could track the day and month of the year.

The Sky-Dweller has a distinctive dial. The primary time zone is told as on any traditional watch, with seconds, minute and hour hands travelling around a circular track of Roman numerals and markers. In an off-centre sub dial, you

will find the second time zone, with a red triangle pointing to the correct hour on a 24-hour wheel. As with many Rolex models, the date is displayed in a Cyclops-enhanced window at 3 o'clock. Now, for something new: the month of the year is indicated by 12 apertures positioned on the hours. Should number eight's box appear coloured-in, usually in red, that would indicate it is August, and so on.

What is particularly clever about the annual calendar complication, which Rolex named Saros, is that it knows how many days each month has and will reset its counter automatically when it hits 30 or 31. The only manual correction that needs to be made is once a year on March 1st to account for February having either 28 or 29 days. The watch's time zone and calendar functions can be controlled and set using the Sky-Dweller's fluted bezel and crown. This is made possible by Rolex's Ring Command system, a complex mechanism made up of about 50 parts.

Cellini and Perpetual 1908

All of the iconic Rolex watches profiled thus far have one thing in common: the model names are all prefixed by Oyster Perpetual. Essentially, each watch uses the brand's trademark Oyster case as a base. The Cellini and Perpetual 1908 collections are different, as these dress watches don't have Oyster cases.

First launched in 1968, the Cellini range is named after Benvenuto Cellini, an Italian goldsmith, sculptor and

OPPOSITE: A steel Sky-Dweller with blue dial and Oyster bracelet.

author who lived in Florence in the 16th century. All of the watches crafted under the Cellini banner are made in gold or platinum.

Less instantly recognisable than the Oyster Perpetual models, the Cellini watches have attracted a fan base that prefers a quieter kind of luxury. Former US president Barack Obama is one of them, having been seen wearing a white gold Cellini Ref. 50509.

Over the years, there have been a number of complications (additional functions) within the range: Time displays the hours, minutes and seconds; Date showcases the date in a sub dial at 3 o'clock; Dual Time displays two time zones. At the top of the range is Moonphase which, as its name suggests, has a complication that illustrates what phase the moon is in throughout the month. This function is driven by a self-winding mechanical movement with a patented moonphase module that remains astronomically accurate for 122 years.

In 2022, Rolex discontinued its Cellini series, and the following year introduced a new dress watch called Perpetual 1908. The first of these watches has a new movement – caliber 7140 – housed inside a gold case on a brown alligator strap. The clean, white dial is decorated with Arabic numerals and a seconds sub dial. It was named 1908 in recognition of the year Rolex registered its trademark in Switzerland.

OPPOSITE: A classic gold Rolex Cellini with ivory gloss dial embossed with Rolex typography, set on a black leather strap.

Forging Partnerships

The world of Rolex stretches far beyond its watchmaking hub in Switzerland. Whether for marketing or philanthropy, the watch brand has built partnerships with other industries and activities to ensure that its name is carried far and wide.

Some are obvious connections, such as sporting events or exploration, while others are a little more abstract, like its support of architecture, film and classical music. Whatever world it dips into, Rolex seems keen to leave a positive legacy. Be it through supporting new creative talent or funding projects that could lead to the preservation of our environment, each partnership has depth and meaning.

Such wide-ranging interests also help to ensure that Rolex retains its crown as the world's most famous watch brand.

OPPOSITE: Swiss tennis player Stanislas Wawrinka plays at the 2014 ATP Monte-Carlo Rolex Masters in Monaco.

Sports

Rolex has had strong ties to the sporting world since its first ambassador, Mercedes Gleitze, swam the English Channel in 1927. In addition to engaging athletes to wear its watches and provide testimonials, the brand has also been a pioneer in sporting sponsorship.

The concept of brands endorsing sporting events as marketing really took off in the early 20th century; one of the first major deals was Coke's sponsorship of the 1928 Olympics.

Rolex was an early supporter of motorsports, positioning its watches on the wrist of 'King of Speed' Sir Malcom Campbell as he broke the World Land Speed Record nine times. It sponsored the Daytona International Speedway racetrack when it opened in 1959, after which its Daytona chronograph is named. Since then, its presence in the motoring world has grown steadily. It has committed to sponsor the Rolex

24 At Daytona, 24 Hours of Le Mans, the FIA World Endurance Championship, and in 2013 it became the official timepiece of Formula 1. Quirkier motoring events it supports include Pebble Beach Concours d'Elegance, The Quail – A Motorsports Gathering, the Rolex Monterey Motorsports Reunion and the Goodwood Revival.

In 1957, Rolex forged a relationship with equestrianism through British show jumper Pat Smythe, who was an ambassador of the brand, and its interest in horses continues to this day. Sponsorships include The Rolex Grand Slam of Show Jumping, a global initiative founded in 2013 that unites the four Majors: The Dutch Masters, the CHIO Aachen, the CSIO Spruce Meadows Masters Tournament and the CHI Geneva.

OPPOSITE: Jérôme Guery rides Quel Homme de Hus during the Rolex Grand Prix Rome show-jumping competition in 2021.

ABOVE: A golfer takes a swing at the 2022 Senior Open presented by Rolex, held in Auchterarder, Scotland.

At many of the sporting events Rolex is associated with, you will often see an iconic Rolex clock with a fluted bezel somewhere in the background. One such event is tennis championship Wimbledon, which the brand first partnered with in 1978 and remains its Official Timekeeper today.

Many tennis stars have fallen for the brand over the years, including Roger Federer, Dominic Thiem, Chris Evert, Garbiñe Muguruza and Jo-Wilfried Tsonga. Rolex is so intertwined with tennis that some tournaments have taken on its name as per the sponsorship agreements: the Rolex Monte-Carlo Masters, the Rolex Shanghai Masters and the Rolex Paris Masters to name a few.

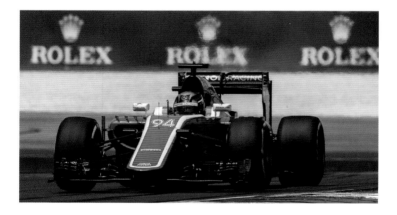

Another area of sports Rolex was keen to align with is sailing, and to do so the watchmaker founded the New York Yacht Club in 1958. Since then, it has sponsored many other yacht clubs and is title sponsor of 15 major international races and regattas, including the annual Rolex Sydney Hobart Yacht Race and the biennial Rolex Fastnet Race, two of the leading offshore contests.

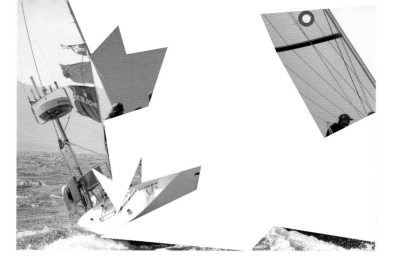

OPPOSITE: Manor
Racing's Pascal
Wehrlein at the 2016
Formula 1 Petronas
Malaysia Grand Prix.

TOP: A team competing
in the 2012 Rolex Swan
Cup sailing race in
Porto Cervo, Italy.

BOTTOM: Tennis player
Rafael Nadal at the
Rolex Monte-Carlo
Masters in 2018.

The Movies

The Jazz Singer, the first talkie (film with sound), and the Rolex Oyster were launched just months apart; an early indicator of the intertwining destinies the watch brand and movie industry would have.

Rolex watches have appeared on the wrists of actors in many films, often as a way to give an additional wordless insight into the character. Sean Connery's James Bond wore an action-ready Submariner in *Dr No* in 1962, while the luxurious gold Day-Date on the wrist of Paul Newman's Fast Eddie in 1987's *The Color of Money* denotes his success as a hustler.

ABOVE: Ben Affleck wears a Deepsea as CIA agent Tony Mendez in *Argo*.

OPPOSITE: Marlon Brando wearing a GMT-Master as Colonel Walter Kurtz in *Apocalypse Now*.

In 2017, Rolex formalised its partnership with the movies by becoming a sponsor of the Academy of Motion Picture Arts and Sciences, the organisation behind the world-famous Oscars awards ceremony. That same year it signed legendary director Martin Scorsese to be an ambassador. He would also become part of the brand's Mentor and Protégé Arts Initiative that pairs established and aspiring talents.

Rolex is now the official watch of the Oscars, and sponsor of its greenroom – a space where nominees and presenters gather before stepping out on stage. Each year, Rolex creates an immersive experience in this room. In 2023, for example, the design was inspired by tropical rainforests, and Rolex used the space to promote its work around environmental preservation.

ABOVE: David Oyelowo wears a gold Rolex Datejust as Martin Luther King, Jr. in *Selma*.

Rolex also sponsors the Governors Awards, given out to those deemed worthy of lifetime achievement awards in cinema. Previous winners have included Michael J. Fox, Elizabeth Taylor, Sidney Poitier, Angelina Jolie and Steven Spielberg. In 2021, the Academy Museum of Motion Pictures opened in Los Angeles, and Rolex was a founding supporter. This temple to cinema has 50,000 square feet of gallery space, including The Rolex Gallery on the third floor.

ABOVE: Michael Caine wore a gold Day-Date as hitman Jack Carter in *Get Carter*.

Expeditions

LEFT: Marine biologist Sylvia Earle prepares to survey coral off the coast of Florida.

OPPOSITE TOP: GMT-Master owner Scott Crossfield was the first person to fly at twice the speed of sound, in an X-15 plane.

OPPOSITE BOTTOM: Rolex adverts celebrating the successful arctic and underwater expeditions of its ambassadors.

Rolex and adventure are synonymous, and some of the stories about its watches accompanying expeditions are legendary. Being on the equipment list for the famous Mount Everest summit made by Tenzing Norgay and Sir Edmund Hillary in 1953 is one example. Others are less well known, but no less important. While that first Everest summit story is the one we all remember, Rolex watches actually accompanied 17 expeditions to the world's highest peaks between 1933 and 1955.

The Arctic and Antarctic hold particularly gruelling challenges for explorers, and some of those who have dared to venture there have used Rolex watches to help them navigate the vast, frozen landscapes. In the early 1990s, Norwegian adventurer Erling Kagge wore an Explorer II while undertaking a solo expedition to the South Pole. It was an incredible journey, with Kagge spending 50 days entirely alone, travelling 815 miles on foot.

Another fan of the Explorer II is high-altitude mountaineer Ed Viesturs, who became the first American to climb the world's 14 peaks over 8,000 metres without supplemental oxygen. Rolex ran an ad campaign celebrating the successes of Viesturs, who became an ambassador of the brand.

Biologist and underwater explorer Sylvia Earle has also partnered with Rolex on expeditions. Over the course of her career, Earle has spent nearly an entire year underwater and once lived on the ocean floor for 14 days for a research project. She is also a champion for the protection of marine life, and, as such, is a close collaborator with Rolex's Perpetual Planet initiative. She has also been part of the Rolex Awards for Enterprise judging panel.

The Arts

While Rolex branding is glaringly obvious at sporting events, its involvement in the arts is more subtle. It describes itself as "moving quietly in the background", providing financial backing to both individuals and institutions for creative pursuits.

The relationship between Rolex and the arts dates back to 1970 when New Zealand soprano Dame Kiri Te Kanawa became the first Rolex arts ambassador. She would be the first of many singers to be connected to the brand, from Italian mezzo-soprano Cecilia Bartoli to Canadian crooner Michael Bublé.

Rolex has also partnered with major cultural institutions, including the Teatro alla Scala in Milan, London's Royal Opera House, the Metropolitan Opera in New York, the Opéra national de Paris, the Teatro Colón in Buenos Aires, and the National Centre for the Performing Arts in Beijing.

The brand has a special relationship with the Vienna Philharmonic orchestra that goes back to 2008, and every year it sponsors its famous New Year's concert. The classical music performance is broadcast live from Musikverein in Vienna to millions of people around the world. Rolex also sponsors its open-air Summer Night Concert that draws 100,000 people to the city's Schönbrunn Palace.

Rolex has engaged with many other artforms, including theatre, literature and film, mostly through its Mentor and Protégé programme. This links leading creatives, including Lin Manuel Miranda, creator of the hit musical *Hamilton*, with emerging artists to support the development of new talent. To mark the 20th anniversary of the Rolex Mentor and

Protégé Arts Initiative, the watchmaker organised an arts festival in Athens in 2023. More than 60 Rolex protégés and mentors shared their achievements and ongoing creative relationships through multidisciplinary performances, exhibitions, readings, screenings, installations and discussions.

ABOVE: The auditorium of the Palais Garnier in Paris, France.

Architecture

Architecture might seem an offbeat interest for a watch brand, but Rolex is deeply involved in this world, which it sees as having parallels to its own in terms of an appreciation for precision and design.

It has built relationships with leading architectural events, including becoming the official timepiece of the Biennale Architettura, part of La Biennale di Venezia. It has also engaged top architects to be part of its Mentor and Protégé programme, including Sir David Adjaye, Sir David Chipperfield, Kazuyo Sejima, Álvaro Siza and Peter Zumthor. Much care is taken over the design of its own buildings, too. It engages top firms including Onsitestudio, Kengo Kuma, SANAA, Michael Graves and Fumihiko to create spaces that are aesthetically provocative. Rolex uses this as an opportunity to strengthen its commitment to its Perpetual Planet initiative by favouring sustainable architects and builds.

OPPOSITE: Lorenzo Quinn's Building Bridges installation at the 58th Venice Biennale.

LEFT: The Jumex contemporary art museum in Mexico City, designed by Sir David Chipperfield.

Philanthropy

While most watch brands have philanthropic activities, or even entire divisions dedicated to philanthropic pursuits, Rolex itself is owned by a charity. Founder Hans Wilsdorf set up the Hans Wilsdorf Foundation in 1945 to commemorate his first wife Florence May Wilsdorf-Crotty, who had passed away the year before. When Wilsdorf died in 1960 he transferred his 100% ownership stake in Rolex to the Foundation.

At that time, five Foundation trustees took control of the company, serving as custodians rather than owners or shareholders. The trustees oversaw the operations at Rolex and ensured that it supported good causes.

The Foundation still owns and controls Rolex today. As a not-for-profit organisation, it uses much of its income to support charitable and social causes, including through its Rolex Awards for Enterprise and Perpetual Planet initiatives.

PREVIOUS: The Hans Wilsdorf Bridge in Geneva, named after Rolex's founder.

RIGHT: Snow-capped mountains in Antarctica.

Enterprise

To mark the 50th anniversary of the Oyster in 1976, the Rolex Awards for Enterprise were launched. In an advert promoting the initiative, the watchmaker said the Awards' aim was to "stimulate new projects, which carry on the tradition of enterprise and achievement associated with the name Rolex".

The first Awards offered to pay 50,000 Swiss francs each to five enterprising souls seeking funding for worthy projects. The competition was originally intended to be a one-off event, but it proved so popular that it returned in 1981, 1983 and 1987, by which point Rolex committed to making it a regular event that now happens every two years.

The type of projects that win the Awards for Enterprise tend to reflect the concerns of the day. In the 1990s, many of the winning pitches were related to environmental concerns, such as monitoring ozone levels, reforestation, reducing CFCs and providing solutions to agricultural problems. In the 2000s, Rolex's judging panel selected projects related to natural disasters caused by climate change and the emergence of unknown diseases.

The technological advances of the Noughties made it possible for the Awards to go global. Potential laureates, the name given to winners, could enter from all over the world, and ceremonies began to be held in multiple cities. In 2010, a new offshoot of the awards, the Young Laureates, was launched with the aim of supporting ideas brought by those aged between 18 and 30.

Since its launch, the Awards have attracted more than 35,500 applications from 190 counties. There have been 155 laureates, ranging in age from 24 to 74. Projects have focused on a wide range of issues, from saving India's rainforests to conflict prevention in Chad, and eradicating malnutrition in Tanzania.

OPPOSITE: Hindou Oumarou Ibrahim's plan to use mapping to reduce climate-related conflict in Chad made her a 2021 Rolex Awards laureate.

RIGHT: An advert for the 1987 Rolex Awards for Enterprise.

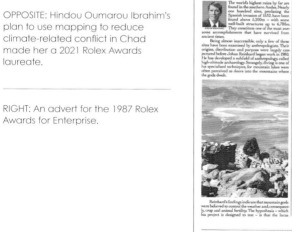

Emerging Talent

Rolex has long been a passionate supporter of the arts, and in 2002 it launched an initiative that would not just deepen its own connection to this world but forge new connections for emerging talents. This was the beginning of the Rolex Mentor & Protégé programme.

The aim of the programme is to find emerging talents in music, film, literature, theatre, visual arts and architecture, and pair them with an inspiring mentor who is well known in the same field. Prospective protégés are not allowed to apply but must instead be nominated by a board made up of artists and arts executives. The board changes every two years to encourage diversity.

Once a protégé has been selected, the leaders of the Mentor & Protégé programme will consult with them to discover what type of mentor would suit them best. It is important to find the right fit as the mentor and protégé must commit to spending a minimum of six weeks together over two years.

Previous mentors have included *The Handmaid's Tale* author Margaret Atwood, who was partnered with English writer Naomi Alderman. The pair soon found common ground, with Atwood challenging and guiding Alderman's writing, and the partnership was so successful that the two women co-wrote a zombie novella for Canadian online literature platform Wattpad.

Rolex provides financial support for protégés to allow them to travel to see their mentors. Protégés can also apply to the programme for funding to facilitate new work. The supportive relationship between Rolex and these rising stars is long lasting, and some creatives who have gone on to have successful careers since being protégés have returned as mentors to coach the next generation.

OPPOSITE: Literary protégé Naomi Alderman with her mentor, the author Margaret Atwood.

RIGHT: Film director and Rolex mentor Martin Scorsese.

Learning

The Rolex Learning Centre in Lausanne, Switzerland, embodies two of the watchmaker's great loves: architecture and learning. The building, which opened in 2010, is part of the Ecole Polytechnique Fédérale de Lausanne (EPFL) and it is open to the public as well as students. It holds a library with 500,000 books, a learning centre and a cultural hub.

The building itself, designed by Japanese firm SANAA, is an architectural marvel. It has no walls, creating 20,000 square meters of uninterrupted space; the idea is to bring multiple disciplines, such as mathematics, engineering and science, together to share knowledge. Rolex's involvement in this project goes beyond providing enough funding to ensure its name is on the building. The watchmaker has a long-standing relationship with EPFL as a research partner, and collaborates with the university when developing new materials and microtechnology to support its watches.

LEFT: Rolex Learning Centre on the EPFL campus in Lausanne, Switzerland.

The Planet

Whereas once Rolex supported expeditions for the sake of pure discovery, the watchmaker now seeks out partners with a deeper mission through its Perpetual Planet initiative. The shift in focus is a reaction to climate change, and expeditions must have a secondary purpose: discovery that will help us to protect or better understand the planet.

A great example of this shift is Mount Everest. In 1953, Rolex equipped members of the climbing team behind Tenzing Norgay and Sir Edmund Hillary's famous summit just to see if the watches would survive the extremes. In 2019, it teamed up with the National Geographic Society to fund an expedition to Everest not simply to measure human endurance, but to learn more about our planet. The climbers' goal was to install the two highest weather stations in the world and collect the highest ice core ever recorded.

LEFT: Clown fish peek
out of a sea anemone.

OPPOSITE: A group
of climbers ascend
Mount Everest.

Other Perpetual Planet initiatives have included the
Tompkins Conservation project to rewild the southwestern
cone of South America, and explorer Alison Criscitiello's
expedition to retrieve an ice core from Canada's highest
summit, Mount Logan.

As well as recording data and restoring nature, Perpetual
Planet initiatives work hard to share awareness of little-
known environmental issues. This was the case with an
expedition called Under The Pole, which sent divers into
the freezing waters of Svalbard, a Norwegian archipelago in
the Arctic Ocean, in search of marine animal forests. These
forests consist of hydrozoa, animals related to jellyfish, and
corals that spend part of their lives attached to the seabed and
resemble flowers. The dives were tough for both the team and
the equipment, but they were rewarded with the discovery of
the first ever identified marine animal forest in the Arctic.

The Legacy

Rolex isn't just any Swiss watch manufacturer; it is the most famous watch brand in the world. Ask anyone on the street if they have heard of Rolex, and the answer will be yes. This legend has been built slowly over more than a century, with its executives careful to link it to all the right initiatives: sports, adventure, precision and innovation. Its legacy, however, is somewhat out of its hands. This is the part of the story written by the fans.

There is always something to keep us interested in Rolex, from its use as a status symbol in celebrity circles and hip hop lyrics, to the mania for certain 'holy grail' models whipped up by competitive collectors and record-breaking auctions.

RIGHT: A gold Rolex Day-Date on sale at a store in Moscow, Russia.

LEFT: A Rolex store
on Gran Via in
Madrid, Spain.

Star Power

A key focus of Rolex's early marketing strategy was to get its watches on famous wrists. In 1947, for example, Hans Wilsdorf gifted British prime minister Winston Churchill the watchmaker's 100,000th certified chronometer, a gold Datejust. Since then, it has become the watch of choice for many well-known faces in music, film, sports and politics.

Indeed, the political world stage has been particularly rich pickings for Rolex, with the Day-Date so popular with world leaders that it picked up the nickname the 'President'. One president to receive but never publicly wear a Day-Date was John F. Kennedy. The reason is that it was gifted to him by his secret lover Marilyn Monroe, and engraved with "Jack, with love as always, from Marilyn."

Rolex's suggestion that every achievement should be marked with a crown rings true in celebrity circles. When tennis player Roger Federer lifted the Wimbledon trophy in 2009, thereby smashing Pete Sampras' all-time Grand Slam record, he wore a Datejust II, and says the watch acts as a reminder of this moment. In 1970, singer Elvis was gifted a gold Rolex King Midas by his concert organiser after selling out the Houston Aerodrome six nights running.

OPPOSITE: Victoria Beckham wears an Everose Cosmograph to the *Viva Forever!* Spice Girls musical press launch in London in 2012.

While many celebrities are Rolex owners – Daniel Craig, Jennifer Aniston, David and Victoria Beckham, Ryan Gosling, Rihanna, Brad Pitt, Tiger Woods and Jennifer Lopez, to name just a few – some stars' watch choices have become legendary. Actors Paul Newman and Steve McQueen are so synonymous with Rolex that they both had models unofficially named after them: the series of 'Paul Newman' Daytonas and a 'Steve McQueen' Explorer.

TOP: Nick Cannon wears a diamond-set Sky-Dweller to host *America's Got Talent* in 2017.

BOTTOM: Cara Delevigne wears a Rolex to the 2014 Toronto International Film Festival.

OPPOSITE: Stormzy wears an Everose 'Rainbow' Daytona Ref 116505 to the 2020 Brit Awards.

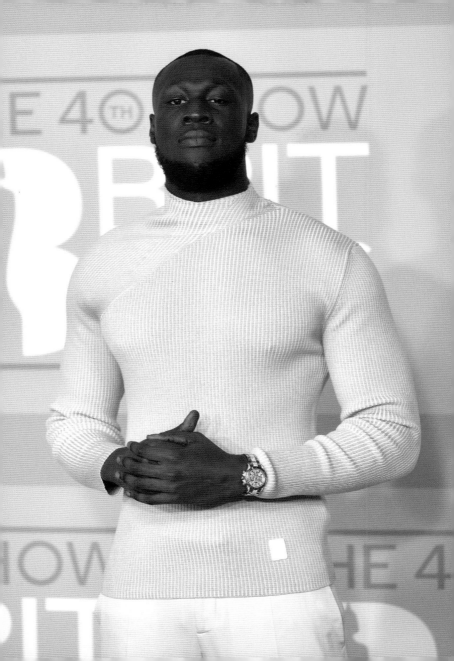

Hip Hop Legends

Horology has become a hot topic in hip hop. If you know what to listen for, you'll hear lyrics about watches in lots of songs, with some artists flexing their watch knowledge by weaving in obscure models and niche brands.

Though these references can often be sophisticated and nuanced, the crux of it is bragging about wealth and possessions. There is no status symbol more universal than a Rolex watch, which is perhaps why it has been referenced in so many songs.

In 2017's 'Plain Jane', A$AP Ferg refers to his "presi plain Jane" in reference to a 'President' Day-Date with no diamonds, bucking the hip hop trend for all-out bling. The rapper later explained that he feels adding diamonds lowers a watch's value and "ruins the art". To do so, he says, is "like taking a Picasso and just saying, 'You know what, I think I should add green on it.'"

A popular Rolex brag in recent years centres on a horological function of Rolex watches: the sweeping seconds hand that travels around the dial smoothly rather than in a ticking motion. Future, Lil Uzi Vert, Iggy Azalea and Travis Scott all have songs stating that their 'Rollies' don't tick; this is often used as an insult to describe another's fake Rolex that does. British artist Skepta pre-empted them all, writing a song called 'Rolex Sweep' in 2009. In the video, he initiated a dance move of the same name in which he circled his arm at full length.

The next generation of artists seem just as entranced with Rolexes. Ayo & Teo, two Gen-Z brothers from Michigan, released a song called Rolex in 2017 that has the lyrics "All I ever wanted was a Rollie" and "My Rollie don't tick tock, it just glide".

OPPOSITE TOP: Photographer Renell Medrano wears a gold Rolex while posing with her partner A$AP Ferg.

OPPOSITE BOTTOM: Pusha T wears a gold Rolex on stage at the 2019 Pitchfork Music Festival in Chicago.

LEFT: A$AP Rocky wears a Rolex while performing at Wireless Festival in London in 2015.

OVERLEAF: Ayo & Teo show off their diamond-set Rolexes at the 2017 BET Awards in Los Angeles.

Rolex at Auction

With Rolexes typically getting snapped up straight off the production line, actually owning one can prove a challenge as there are often long waiting lists. This is perhaps why there is a bustling secondary market, with pre-owned dealers serving up a wide selection of vintage and nearly new timepieces.

The most exceptional examples of Rolexes can be found racking up the bids at auction houses such as Sotheby's and Christie's. This is where the very rare, and therefore incredibly expensive, models will be sold to a global audience.

The highest price ever paid for a Rolex at auction was reached in 2017, and it has yet to be beaten. The model in question was a 1968 Paul Newman Rolex Oyster Cosmograph Daytona Ref. 6239 that was owned by the actor Paul Newman. It had been gifted to him by his wife, Joanne Newman, while he was acting in the film *Winning*.

The price? When the final hammer blow fell at Phillips auction house in New York, bidding stopped at $17.75 million. This makes it the third-most expensive watch ever sold at auction. The top two slots are held by Patek Philippe for a Grandmaster Chime Ref. 6300A-010 that sold in 2019 for $31 million at Christie's, and the 2014 sale of a 1932 Henry Graves Supercomplication for $23.98 million at Sotheby's.

Another major auction moment for Rolex came the year after the sale of Paul Newman's watch, again at Phillips auction house. This time, bidders were vying for a super-rare 18-carat white gold Oyster Cosmograph Ref. 6265, nicknamed 'The Unicorn'. It was donated by legendary watch collector John Goldberger to raise funds for charity Children Action. The final hammer price was $6.5 million.

OPPOSITE: Geoffroy Ader, former Sotheby's European head of watches, holds a 1972 'Paul Newman' Cosmograph Daytona.

ABOVE: A rare 1972 British Royal Navy-issued Submariner Ref. 5513, sold at Bonhams in 2019.

Holy Grails

Rolexes tend to be a good investment, but what sets a watch apart to make it highly collectible, and therefore likely to go up in value? The answer is rarity or provenance. Watch collectors are constantly in search of the unusual, and demand sets prices.

This extends to weird and wonderful examples, not just the best Rolexes. The so-called Tropical dials of the 1950s and 1960s are proof of this. Exposure to UV light caused the black dials to turn brown, which should have rendered them faulty, but for watch collectors hunting for Rolexes nobody else has, they are appealing.

The same goes for discontinued lines and early editions, such as the Submariner Ref. 6204 with its lack of crown guards. Or just incredibly limited lines like the Split-Seconds Chronograph Ref. 4113 of which only 12 were made in 1942.

LEFT: A GMT with Dubai ruler Sheikh Mohammed bin Rashid Al Maktoum's signature on the dial, sold for $162,000 at Christie's in 2018.

OPPOSITE: A gold and diamond Day-Date that belonged to Elvis was auctioned at Christie's in 2012.

Provenance – meaning who owned the watch – can also add some zeros the price. A good example is the 1972 GMT Master Ref. 1675 that Marlon Brando wore as Colonel Kurtz in the film *Apocolypse Now*, and into the case of which he hand-carved his name. The watch would have cost a couple of hundred dollars new, but when it came up for auction at Phillips in 2019, it sold for $1.95 million.

Rolex fans have coined nicknames for many of the most coveted models and features. Particular GMT-Master II models with black and blue Cerachrom bezels are referred to as 'Batman', or 'Batgirl' if paired with a Jubilee bracelet. A Bart Simpson is a Submariner from the 1960s that has a gilt-printed coronet on the crown that some think looks like the cartoon character's hair. Bubbleback refers to the curved ovular caseback of Oyster Perpetuals made in the 1930s to 1950s. Dig into one of the many watch forums online and you'll find more.

RIGHT: The caseback
of Elvis's watch
auctioned at Christie's
in 2012, engravec with
a personal message
from his manager Col.
Tom Parker who gifted
it to the signer. The
relationship between
the two men was
documented in the
2022 Baz Luhrmann
film *Elvis*.

A Watchmaking Legend

The fact that Rolex still can't keep up with demand for its watches more than a century after its launch is testament to its strength. Collectors show little signs of falling out of love with the brand, making its watches both a status symbol for now and a solid investment for the future.

Rolex started its life as a disruptive innovator, creating never-before-seen complications and functions. It has cooled somewhat in recent decades, relying on updating its tried-and-tested roster of Oyster Perpetual spin offs, letting other brands charge ahead with more provocative horology.

What it has done instead is bolster its manufacturing capabilities through acquisition and investment. The look of a new Day-Date might not be wildly different to a vintage model from the 1980s, but what has changed is that all its components, from the movement to the gold used to craft the bracelet, have been produced in house by Rolex. And this perfectionism is what appeals to true watch fans. While other manufacturers might offer up flashier, more exciting launches, Rolex is pleasingly steadfast.

You will now find Rolex watches stocked at more than 1,800 stores around the globe, the majority of which will have long waiting lists for the most coveted models. And for those who are yet to get to the top of those lists, there is a world of vintage Rolex watches just waiting to be discovered, with plenty of associated online forums connecting enthusiasts and sharing knowledge.

Discussing his ambitions for his watch brand, Hans Wilsdorf once said: "We want to be the first in the field, and Rolex should be seen as the one and only – the best." In the eyes of many watch fans, he has certainly succeeded.

OPPOSITE: A Rolex store in Dublin, Ireland.

RIGHT: A Rolex clock in Singapore, in front of a billboard for the brand.

LEFT: A Rolex sign on Nathan Road in Hong Kong, a famous shopping street in the Chinese city that is known as the 'Golden Mile'.

Image Credits

Page 5 Robert Way/Shutterstock; 7 Vladimir Zhupanenko/ Shutterstock; 8 Album/Alamy Stock Photo; 10-11 ullstein bild Dtl./Contributor/Getty; 13 (t) Dominic Byrne/Alamy Stock Photo, (b) Science & Society Picture Library/Contributor/ Getty; 14 (t) ullstein bild Dtl./Contributor/Getty, (b) ullstein bild Dtl./Contributor/Getty; 16 Philip Hartley/Alamy Stock Photo; 17 pio3/Shutterstock; 18 UPI/Alamy Stock Photo; 19 Allstar Picture Library Limited/Alamy Stock Photo; 20 (l) Jeff Morgan 14/Alamy Stock Photo, (r) Retro AdArchives/ Alamy Stock Photo; 21 Portal Satova/Shutterstock; 22-23 Prateep oun/Shutterstock; 24 LEVANTEMEDIA/Shutterstock; 25 Jitjaroen Channarong/Shutterstock; 26-27 Travel Stock/ Shutterstock; 29 (l) PA Images/Alamy Stock Photo, (r) De Luan/Alamy Stock Photo; 30 Heritage Image Partnership Ltd/ Alamy Stock Photo; 31 US Air Force Photo/Alamy Stock Photo; 33 D and S Photography Archives/Alamy Stock Photo; 34 Patti McConville/Alamy Stock Photo; 35 Associated Press/Alamy Stock Photo; 36 Adam Bignell/Unsplash; 37 Portal Satova/ Shutterstock; 39 Portal Satova/Shutterstock; 40 Casey Connell/Unsplash; 41 i viewfinder/Shutterstock; 42-43 Filipp Romanovski/Unsplash; 44 pio3/Shutterstock; 45 Norjipin Saidi/Shutterstock; 46 Science & Society Picture Library/ Contributor/Getty; 49 Yash Parashar/Unsplash; 50 (t) Jitjaroen Channarong/Shutterstock, (b) i viewfinder/Shutterstock; 52-53 RetekG/Alamy Stock Photo; 54-55 Sorbis/Shutterstock; 56-

57 olrat/Shutterstock; 58 Jitjaroen Channarong/Shutterstock; 59 Jitjaroen Channarong/Shutterstock; 60 FXQuadro/Alamy; 63 Rene Paik/Alamy Stock Photo; 65 Grzegorz Czapski/ Alamy Stock Photo; 66-67 Rene Paik/Alamy Stock Photo; 68 jealfish Ping/Shutterstock; 69 Jitjaroen Channarong/ Shutterstock; 70-71 dpa picture alliance/Alamy Stock Photo; 73 andersphoto/Shutterstock; 74-75 pio3/Shutterstock; 75-77 Enjoy The Life/Shutterstock; 78 @Misakyanovich/Unsplash; 81 Millenary Watches/Unsplash; 82 andersphoto/Shutterstock; 84 Portal Satova/Shutterstock; 87 music phone/Shutterstock; 88 Portal Satova/Shutterstock; 91 Portal Satova/Shutterstock; 92 A. Astes/Alamy Stock Photo; 95 Getty Images Europe; 96-97 A. Astes/Alamy Stock Photo; 99 naskopi/Shutterstock; 100-101 andersphoto/Shutterstock; 102 naskopi/Shutterstock; 105 Jitjaroen Channarong/Shutterstock; 106-107 DPPI Media/Alamy Stock Photo; 108 Gennaro Leonardi Photos/ Shutterstock; 109 Matt Hooper/Shutterstock; 110 Nufa Qaiesz/ Shutterstock; 111 (t) Lpuddori/Shutterstock, (b) FRANCESCO PANUNZIO/Shutterstock; 112 Photo 12/Alamy Stock Photo; 113 AJ Pics/Alamy Stock Photo; 114 Photo 12/Alamy Stock Photo; 115 Allstar Picture Library Ltd/Alamy Stock Photo; 116 Associated Press/Alamy Stock Photo; 117 (t) stock imagery/ Alamy Stock photo, (b) Risky Walls/Alamy Stock Photo; 119 STLJB/Shutterstock; 120 Simlinger/Shutterstock; 121 Chepe Nicoli/Shutterstock; 122-123 Yannick Martinez/Shutterstock; 124-125 Goinyk Production/Shutterstock; 126 Sipa US/Alamy; 127 Risky Walls/Alamy Stock Photo; 128 Colin McConnell/ Contributor/Getty; 129 Dfree/Shutterstock; 130-131 Mihai-Bogdan Lazar/Shutterstock; 132 Vixit/Shutterstock; 134-135 Papin Lab/Shutterstock; 136-137 tomsmdt/Shutterstock 138

RIGHT: The iconic Rolex crown motif on one of the brand's signature green watch boxes.